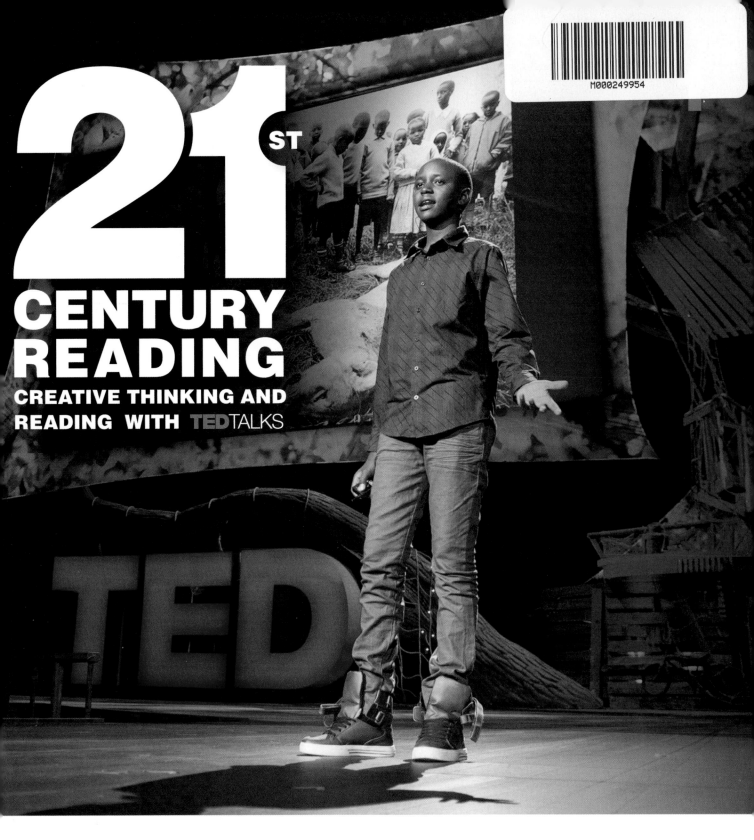

21ST CENTURY READING

CREATIVE THINKING AND READING WITH TEDTALKS

Robin Longshaw • Laurie Blass

NATIONAL GEOGRAPHIC LEARNING

CENGAGE Learning·

Australia • Brazil • Japan • Korea • Mexico • Singapore • Spain • United Kingdom • United States

**21st Century Reading Student Book 1
Creative Thinking and Reading with
TED Talks**

Robin Longshaw

Laurie Blass

Publisher: Andrew Robinson

Executive Editor: Sean Bermingham

Development Editor: Tom Jefferies

Editorial Assistant: Dylan Mitchell

Director of Global Marketing: Ian Martin

Executive Marketing Manager: Ben Rivera

Media Researcher: Leila Hishmeh

Director of Content and Media Production:
Michael Burggren

Production Manager: Daisy Sosa

Senior Print Buyer: Mary Beth Hennebury

Cover and Interior Designers: Scott Baker
and Aaron Opie

Cover Image: Richard Turere, inventor,
at TED2013: The Young, The Wise,
The Undiscovered. Tuesday,
February 26, 2013, Long Beach, CA.
©James Duncan Davidson/TED

Composition: Cenveo® Publisher Services

Student Book
ISBN 13: 978-1-305-26459-5

National Geographic Learning/Cengage Learning
20 Channel Center Street
Boston, MA 02210
USA

Cengage Learning is a leading provider of customised learning solutions with office locations around the globe, including Singapore, the United Kingdom, Australia, Mexico, Brazil and Japan. Locate our local office at **international.cengage.com/region**

Cengage Learning products are represented in Canada by Nelson Education Ltd.

Visit National Geographic Learning online at **NGL.Cengage.com**
Visit our corporate website at **www.cengage.com**

Printed in the United States of America
Print Number: 01   Print Year: 2014

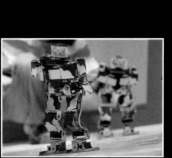

SCOPE AND SEQUENCE

Unit/Theme	Lesson A Reading	Reading Skills	Critical Thinking
1 **LIFE CHANGES** *Interdisciplinary*	*The Power to Change* Biographical article	• Understanding sequence words • Creating a timeline	• Interpreting a person's statement • Reflecting on own experience
2 **TEAM POWER** *Business / Leadership*	*The Marshmallow Challenge* Research article	• Identifying main ideas in paragraphs • Identifying supporting details	• Interpreting a person's statement • Reflecting on own experience
3 **OCEAN WONDERS** *Life Science*	*Messages from the Sea* Scientific article	• Identifying purpose • Identifying referents	• Inferring meaning from context • Evaluating and justifying an opinion
4 **WHAT WE WEAR** *Sociology / Fashion*	*The Science of Style* Research report	• Making connections • Understanding a process	• Inferring reasons • Reflecting on own experience
5 **MOMENTS AND MEMORIES** *Psychology / History*	*Preserving the Past* Biographical article	• Identifying approximate numbers • Understanding visuals	• Inferring meaning from context • Reflecting on own experience
6 **BUILDING SOLUTIONS** *Architecture and Design*	*Living Spaces* Magazine-style article	• Organizing supporting details • Understanding reasons	• Synthesizing information • Analyzing problems
7 **ROADS TO FAME** *Communication / Sociology*	*Going Viral* Magazine-style article	• Scanning for numbers • Understanding a graph • Identifying transition words	• Inferring attitude • Reflecting on own experience
8 **FACE OFF** *Conservation / Engineering*	*Lions Killed Near Nairobi* News report	• Identifying cause and effect • Visualizing details • Understanding infographics	• Reasoning and justifying an opinion • Reflecting on possible solutions
9 **COMMUNITY VOICES** *Visual Arts / Sociology*	*Art in the Community* Biographical article	• Understanding a paragraph's purpose • Understanding references	• Interpreting a reaction • Making predictions • Applying ideas to other contexts
10 **ROBOTS AND US** *Technology / Robotics*	*Robots Like Us* Scientific article	• Identifying main and supporting ideas in paragraphs • Making comparisons	• Evaluating pros and cons • Reflecting on own experience

Lesson B	TED Talks	Academic Skills	Critical Thinking	Project
	Try Something New for 30 Days Matt Cutts	• Understanding main ideas and key details • Recognizing attitude • Identifying facts and opinions	• Evaluating challenges • Reflecting on own experience	• Planning a 30-day challenge
	Build a Tower, Build a Team Tom Wujec	• Understanding main ideas and key details • Understanding stages in a process • Summarizing main ideas	• Inferring reasons • Reflecting on personal strengths • Applying ideas	• Designing a team-building task
	Underwater Astonishments David Gallo	• Understanding main ideas and key details • Recognizing tone and message • Synthesizing information using a Venn diagram	• Questioning a speaker • Reflecting on own experience	• Researching and presenting examples of adaptation
	Wearing Nothing New Jessi Arrington	• Understanding main ideas and key details • Recognizing point of view • Comparing messages	• Interpreting statements • Reflecting on personal style	• Researching for a poster session on clothing
	One Second Every Day Cesar Kuriyama	• Understanding main ideas and key details • Recognizing a message • Identifying true statements	• Interpreting a statement • Synthesizing ideas • Evaluating an argument • Reflecting on own experience	• Planning a media show about memories
	Ingenious Homes in Unexpected Places Iwan Baan	• Understanding main ideas and key details • Summarizing ideas using a concept map • Recognizing attitude	• Inferring reasons • Applying ideas to own experience	• Researching for a talk about an unusual structure
	Why Videos Go Viral Kevin Allocca	• Understanding main ideas and key details • Recognizing a message • Summarizing ideas using a concept map	• Applying ideas to other contexts • Reflecting on reasons	• Researching and presenting a viral video
	My Invention that Made Peace with Lions Richard Turere	• Understanding main ideas and key details • Recognizing tone and message • Summarizing ideas using a process diagram	• Making predictions • Interpreting meaning • Questioning a speaker	• Researching and presenting on human–animal conflict
	Before I Die, I Want To… Candy Chang	• Understanding main ideas and key details • Making predictions • Recognizing point of view	• Interpreting a speaker's statement • Making predictions • Synthesizing and applying ideas	• Conducting a survey about your community
	The Rise of Personal Robots Cynthia Breazeal	• Understanding main ideas and key details • Understanding sequence • Summarizing main ideas	• Analyzing problems	• Creating a design for a new robot

WHAT IS 21ST CENTURY READING?

21ST CENTURY READING develops essential knowledge and skills for learners to succeed in today's global society. The series teaches core academic language skills and incorporates 21st century themes and skills such as global awareness, information literacy, and critical thinking.

Each unit of 21st Century Reading has three parts:

- **READ** about a 21st century topic—such as social robots and viral videos—in Lesson A.
- **LEARN** more about the topic by viewing an authentic TED Talk in Lesson B.
- **EXPLORE** the topic further by completing a collaborative research project.

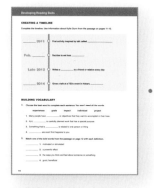

VOCABULARY BUILDING

READING SKILLS

LANGUAGE SKILLS

Strategies for understanding key ideas, language use, and purpose.

BUSINESS AND TECHNOLOGY

GLOBAL AWARENESS

21ST CENTURY THEMES

Interdisciplinary topics that affect everyone in a global society

LEARNING SKILLS

The "4 C's" that all learners need for success in a complex world.

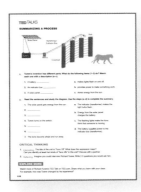

CRITICAL THINKING AND COMMUNICATION

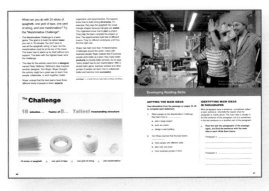

CREATIVITY AND COLLABORATION

21ST CENTURY LITERACIES

The ability to deal with information in a variety of modern formats and media.

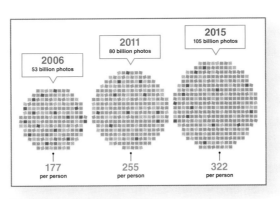

VISUAL LITERACY

INFORMATION AND MEDIA LITERACIES

➜ For more on 21st century learning, see **www.p21.org/** and **21foundation.com/**

LIFE
CHANGES

GOALS

IN THIS UNIT, YOU WILL:

- Read about someone who changed her life.
- Learn about 30-day challenges.
- Explore ways to change your life.

THINK AND DISCUSS

1. Why do people make changes in their lives?

2. In your opinion, what kinds of changes are difficult to make? What kinds of changes are easy to make?

Hikers climb Mount Kilimanjaro, Tanzania.

PRE-READING

A. Read the information in the "What is TED?" feature on page 12. Write your answers to the questions. Then discuss your answers with a partner.

1. What does TED do?

   _____

2. How many countries have held TEDx events?

   _____

B. Look at the passage's title, headings, photos, and captions (pages 11–12). Then answer the question below. Read the passage to check your ideas.

   What do you think the passage is about?

   a. How change can be difficult

   b. How TED events happen all over the world

   c. How TED Talks inspire people

C. Have you ever seen a presentation or talk that changed you in some way? Discuss with a partner.

A large audience listens to Saskia Sassen, a writer and sociologist, giving a TED Talk in 2013.

THE POWER TO CHANGE

Since its first event in 1984, TED has aimed to inspire people around the world by sharing powerful ideas.

1 In 2011, Kylie Dunn, a writer from Australia, decided to shake up her life. Every month for a year, she decided to try two new activities. In February 2012, for example, one of her **goals** was to eat less meat for 30 days. Later, she wrote a letter to a friend or relative every day for a month. In just 12 months, she changed her life in more than 20 different ways.

Kylie Dunn

A YEAR OF CHANGE

2 Dunn was **inspired** to try her **project** after watching a TED Talk by Matt Cutts. To get ideas for activities, she watched hundreds of other TED Talks. Her first activity, in November 2011, was inspired by Jessi Arrington's talk "Wear Nothing New." Dunn tried each activity for 30 days, and then wrote about her **experiences** in a blog called "My Year of TED."

3 Finally, when her project was over, Dunn talked about her experiences at a TEDx conference in Hobart, Australia. Dunn's talk in January 2014 inspired other people to change their **attitudes** and their lives. Before her project, Dunn says, she didn't think she had the courage to change her life. The project showed her she had more strength than she thought.

A MILLION STORIES

4 "People who watch TED Talks . . . end up shifting their view of the future," says Chris Anderson, the curator of TED. He says that TED's goal isn't to make a single big change. TED's **impact** is the millions of stories of small changes. **Individual** changes like Kylie Dunn's are happening every day. Together, these changes have the power to change the future in a **positive** way. As Anderson explains, "Instead of thinking of [the future] as an unstoppable force . . . [people can] play a part in shaping it."

---

courage: *n.* a willingness to do something that is difficult or dangerous

shifting: *v.* moving, changing

view: *n.* an opinion or way of thinking about something

curator: *n.* a person who selects and manages a collection of art, videos, etc.

What is TED?

TED has a simple goal: to spread great ideas. Every year, hundreds of presenters share ideas at TED events around the world. Millions of people watch TED Talks online. The talks inspire many people to change their attitudes and their lives.

SPREADING IDEAS WORLDWIDE

 Over **10,000** TEDx events in **167** countries

 Over **1,800** TEDTALKS recorded

 TEDTALKS translated into **105** languages

 Over **1,000,000,000** views of TEDTALKS at **TED.com**

Source: TED 2014

Organizers help set up a TEDx event in Sydney, Australia.

Developing Reading Skills

GETTING THE MAIN IDEAS

Choose the best answer for each question. Use information from the passage on pages 11–12.

1. What is the main idea of the passage?

   a. Many people watch TED Talks online.

   b. People can try different things for 30 days.

   c. TED Talks spread ideas that can change lives.

2. Why did Kylie Dunn do her "year of TED"?

   a. She was inspired by a TED Talk.

   b. She started a new job at TED.

   c. She needed a new challenge.

3. What does Chris Anderson say about the future?

   a. Small changes can have a positive impact on the future.

   b. Most people are afraid of what will happen in the future.

   c. People should make a single big change.

UNDERSTANDING SEQUENCE WORDS

When writing about a process, writers use sequence words to organize their ideas. Sequence words include: *first, second, third, next, later, then, before, after,* and *finally*. Sometimes writers do not write all parts of the process in chronological (time) order. It is important to notice sequence words as you read.

A. **Find and circle the sequence words in paragraphs 1–3 on page 12.**

B. **Complete the paragraph with the best sequence word. Use the information from the passage.**

   TED _____ began to put videos of TED Talks
   ₁

   on the Internet in 2006. Five years _____, writer
   ₂

   Kylie Dunn decided to change her life _____
   ₃

   watching a TED Talk by Matt Cutts. She watched a lot of

   talks to get ideas. _____, she used these ideas
   ₄

   to decide her projects. When her projects were

   _____ over, she gave her own TED Talk.
   ₅

CREATING A TIMELINE

Complete the timeline. Use information about Kylie Dunn from the passage on pages 11–12.

_____ 2011 — First activity inspired by talk called _____

Feb. _____ — Decides to eat less _____

Late 2012 — Writes a _____ to a friend or relative every day

_____ 2014 — Gives a talk at a TEDx event in Hobart, _____

BUILDING VOCABULARY

A. Choose the best word to complete each sentence. You won't need all the words.

experiences   goals   impact   individual   project

1. Many people have _____ or objectives that they want to accomplish in their lives.

2. A(n) _____ is carefully planned work that has a special purpose.

3. Something that is _____ is related to one person or thing.

4. _____ are event that happens to you.

B. Match one of the bold words from the passage on page 12 with each definition.

_____ 1. motivated or stimulated

_____ 2. a powerful effect

_____ 3. the ways you think and feel about someone or something

_____ 4. good, beneficial

GETTING MEANING FROM CONTEXT

A. **After watching a TED Talk, Kylie Dunn says she was inspired to "shake up her life." What did she mean by this? Choose the best answer.**

    a. She decided to move to a different country.

    b. She decided to make changes in her life.

    c. She decided to write a book about life changes.

B. **Can you think of another person who decided to "shake up their life"? Who or what inspired that person?**

_____

_____

_____

_____

CRITICAL THINKING

1. Interpreting. Chris Anderson says that many people think the future is "an unstoppable force." What do you think he means? Choose the best answer.

    a. People believe the future is too far away.

    b. People think they can't change the future.

    c. People feel excited about the future.

2. Reflecting. Who or what has inspired you to make a change in your life? What change(s) did you make?

_____

_____

EXPLORE MORE

Read Kylie Dunn's "My Year of TED" blog at blog.TED.com. What other changes did she make? Share what you learned with the class.

Artwork by Kylie Dunn's brother, Matthew Dunn, to accompany one of her challenges.
Dunn spent 30 days trying to figure out what she wanted to do with her life.

TEDTALKS

TRY SOMETHING NEW FOR 30 DAYS

MATT CUTTS Software engineer, TED speaker

In 2009, Matt Cutts decided to make some changes to his lifestyle.

Cutts was inspired by documentary filmmaker Morgan Spurlock. Spurlock decided to eat only fast food for 30 days to see how his body changed—mostly in bad ways. Cutts followed the same 30-day time period but made positive changes to his life. He blogged about what he learned in the process. Cutts not only changed his life, he inspired many other people to change their lives, too.

lifestyle: *n.* a way of living, a person's habits

documentary: *n.* a movie or TV program about real people or events

In this lesson, you are going to watch Cutts's TED Talk. Use the information above about Cutts to answer each question.

1. When did Matt Cutts begin to make changes in his life?

2. Who inspired Cutts to change?

3. How did Cutts tell people about his project?

Cutts's **idea worth spreading** is that we can become better versions of ourselves if we try something new—30 days at a time.

TEDTALKS

PREVIEWING

A. Scan the excerpt below from Cutts's TED Talk. What should you think about when choosing a 30-day challenge?

_____

_____

B. Complete the excerpt using the words below. Then watch () Cutts's TED Talk, and check your answers.

idea   something   time   try   years

« A few _____ ago, I felt like I was stuck in a rut. So I decided to follow in the footsteps of the great
                  1

American philosopher, Morgan Spurlock, and try _____ new for 30 days. The _____ is actually
                                                          2   3

pretty simple. Think about something you've always wanted to add to your life, and _____ it for the
                                                                                                    4

next 30 days. It turns out, 30 days is just about the right amount of _____ to add a new habit or
                                                                                    5

subtract a habit—like watching the news—from your life. »

stuck in a rut: _idiom_ to feel trapped or bored by routine   **turns out:** _v._ happens, ends, or develops in a particular way

The average American consumes over 600 teaspoons of sugar a month. For a 30-Day Challenge, Matt Cutts set out to survive a month without any.

18

GETTING THE MAIN IDEAS

What is Cutts's talk mainly about? Check (✓) the four ideas he mentions.

- [ ] **a.** It is possible to do anything for 30 days if you really want to.
- [ ] **b.** If you take a picture every day, you become a good photographer.
- [ ] **c.** Completing difficult challenges made Cutts feel more confident.
- [ ] **d.** Small life changes are easier than big life changes.
- [ ] **e.** When you complete 30-day challenges, you remember more about your life.

UNDERSTANDING KEY DETAILS

Watch (▶) Cutts's talk again. Choose the best answer for each question about Cutts's challenges.

1. His daily photo helped Cutts _____.

   a. improve his photography skills

   b. visit interesting places

   c. remember more

2. Cutts _____ after his challenges.

   a. was healthier

   b. was more adventurous

   c. met many interesting people

3. Cutts wanted to write a novel in 30 days. He _____.

   a. became a famous author

   b. wrote about 1,700 words every day

   c. wrote an excellent book

4. Cutts stopped eating sugar for 30 days. Then he _____.

   a. started eating sugar again

   b. never ate sugar again

   c. felt very healthy

RECOGNIZING THE SPEAKER'S ATTITUDE

Read the excerpt from Cutts's talk. Then choose the best answer for each question.

❝ So here's my question to you: What are you waiting for? I guarantee you the next 30 days are going to pass whether you like it or not, so why not think about something you have always wanted to try and give it a shot for the next 30 days? ❞

---

give (something) a shot: *n.* to try something

1. Which statement best matches Cutts's attitude about 30-day challenges?

   a. He's glad the challenges are over.

   b. The 30-day challenges only made a small difference.

   c. He feels good that he tried the 30-day challenges.

2. What does Cutts suggest to the audience?

   a. They should think carefully before they try a 30-day challenge.

   b. They should tell other people about 30-day challenges.

   c. They should use the next 30 days to try a new challenge.

For one of his 30-day challenges, Matt Cutts climbed up Mt. Kilimanjaro, Tanzania.

IDENTIFYING FACTS AND OPINIONS

Read these statements from Matt Cutts. Decide whether they are facts or his opinions. Write F (Fact) or O (Opinion) for each one.

1. _____ "I ended up hiking up Mt. Kilimanjaro, the highest mountain in Africa."

2. _____ "If you really want something badly enough, you can do anything for 30 days."

3. _____ "Every November, tens of thousands of people try to write their own 50,000-word novel."

4. _____ "The secret [to writing a novel] is not to go to sleep until you've written your words for the day."

5. _____ "There's nothing wrong with big, crazy challenges."

CRITICAL THINKING

1. Evaluating. How likely would you be able to achieve these challenges in 30 days? Rank them from 1 (most likely) to 5 (least likely). Share your ideas with a partner.

   _____ Climb a high mountain   _____ Learn to play a new sport

   _____ Run a marathon (42-km race)   _____ Write a book

   _____ Stop eating meat

2. Reflecting. Cutts says that small lifestyle changes are easier than big changes. What is an example of a small change you can make?

_____

EXPLORE MORE

Read more about Matt Cutts at TED.com. What other 30-day challenges has he completed? Share what you learned with your class.

Project

A. **You are going to design a 30-day challenge for yourself.**

1. Think about the 30-day challenges that Matt Cutts and Kylie Dunn did. Brainstorm two or three possible challenges in each category below.

Health   *Run three times a week*   _____

_____   _____

Creativity   *Take piano lessons*   _____

_____   _____

Relationships   *Talk to all my neighbors*   _____

_____   _____

2. Choose one 30-day challenge from your brainstorm. Answer the questions below to plan it.

- When will you begin?
- How much time do you need each day?
- What time of day is best for you to do the activity?
- Who can help you with your challenge?
- How will you share your challenge with other people?

B. **Work with a partner. Present your 30-day challenge. Use the following steps.**

- Explain your challenge.
- As you listen to other pairs, take notes.
- At the end, review your notes.
- Ask any questions you have about the challenges the other pairs presented.
- Do you want to change or add anything in your own 30-day challenge?

EXPLORE MORE

Search TED.com for the playlist "A Better You." Learn about other people who have changed their lives. Share what you learned in class.

TEAM
POWER

GOALS

IN THIS UNIT, YOU WILL:

- Read about an unusual team game.
- Learn about the factors that can make a team successful.
- Explore ways to work together.

THINK AND DISCUSS

1. Where can you find people working as part of a team?

2. Some teams work better than other teams. Why do you think that is?

Participants called 'Castellers' form a human tower during La Mercè Festival in Barcelona, Spain.

Lesson A

PRE-READING

A. Look at the pictures on pages 26 and 27. Write answers to the questions below. Then discuss your answers with a partner.

    1. What are the people doing? What materials are they using?

    _____

    _____

    _____

    2. What do you think the Marshmallow Challenge is?

    _____

    _____

    _____

B. Read the first sentence of each paragraph on page 26. Choose the best answer to the question below. Then read the whole passage to check your ideas.

What is the passage about?

    a. How business people play a team game.

    b. How a man designed a team game.

    c. How people work together in a team game.

THE MARSHMALLOW CHALLENGE

"Every project has its own Marshmallow," according to designer Tom Wujec. The Marshmallow Challenge helps people understand what he means.

What can you do with 20 sticks of spaghetti, one yard of tape, one yard of string, and one marshmallow? Try the "Marshmallow Challenge"!

1   The Marshmallow Challenge is a team game. The goal is to build the tallest **tower** you can in 18 minutes. You don't have to use all the spaghetti, string, or tape, but the marshmallow must be at the top of the tower. The tower has to stand up by itself without any support. The team with the highest tower wins the challenge.

2   The idea for the activity came from a **designer** named Peter Skillman. Skillman's idea inspired another designer, Tom Wujec. Wujec thought the activity might be a great way to learn how people collaborate, or work together, better.

3   Wujec noticed that the best teams have three different kinds of people in them: **experts**, organizers, and experimenters. The experts know how to build strong **structures**. For example, they tape the spaghetti into small triangle shapes because triangles are **stable**. The organizers know how to **plan** a project. They help the team complete the project on time. The experimenters build lots of different towers. They try different prototypes until they find the right one.

4   Wujec has held more than 70 Marshmallow Challenges around the world—many with business people. Wujec realized that if business people work better as a team, they make better **products** or provide better services. As he says, "every project has its own marshmallow." With a simple team game, business workers and other groups of people can learn how to collaborate better and become more **successful**.

---

prototype: *n.* a model that you make before building something

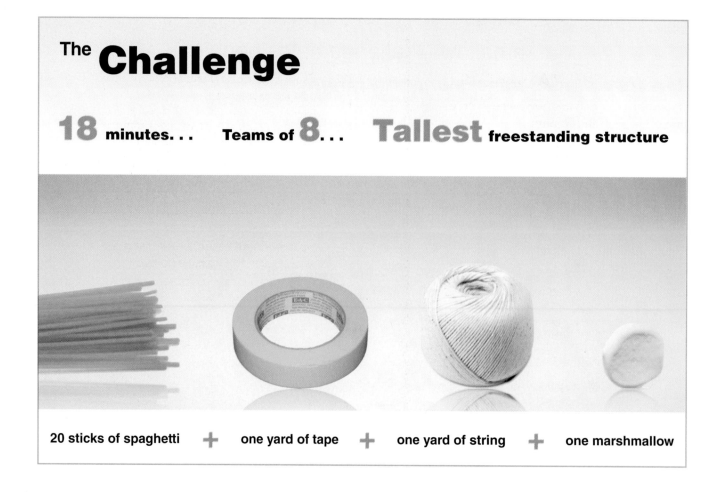

The **Challenge**

18 minutes. . .   Teams of **8**. . .   **Tallest** freestanding structure

20 sticks of spaghetti ✛ **one yard of tape** ✛ **one yard of string** ✛ **one marshmallow**

A team participates in the Marshmallow Challenge.

Developing Reading Skills

GETTING THE MAIN IDEAS

Use information from the passage on pages 25–26 to complete each statement.

1. When people do the Marshmallow Challenge, they learn how to _____.

   a. plan a large project

   b. work as a team

   c. design a real building

2. Tom Wujec learned that the best teams _____.

   a. have people with different skills

   b. plan only one tower

   c. have business people in them

IDENTIFYING MAIN IDEAS IN PARAGRAPHS

Most paragraphs have a sentence—sometimes called a *topic sentence*—that tells the reader what the paragraph is mainly about. This main idea is usually in the first sentence of the paragraph, but it is sometimes in the last sentence or in another part of the paragraph.

A. **Read the last two paragraphs of the passage again, and find the sentence with the main idea in each. Write them below.**

Paragraph 3: _____

_____

_____

Paragraph 4: _____

_____

_____

B. The paragraph below describes the Marshmallow Challenge. The sentences are not in the correct order. First, find and underline the topic sentence. Then put the sentences in order by numbering them 1–4.

_____. They have to finish in 18 minutes. _____. The Marshmallow Challenge is a great activity
a   b

for teaching teams to work together. _____. People can then use their new collaboration skills
c

in their real job. _____. In the activity, teams work to build a tower with unusual materials.
d

IDENTIFYING SUPPORTING DETAILS

Complete the mind map using the words and phrases below. Refer to paragraphs 3 and 4 of the passage on page 26.

a. makes products

b. strong structures

c. more than 70

d. plan projects

e. try different

f. provide better services

BUILDING VOCABULARY

A. Use *bold* words from the passage on pages 25–26 to complete each definition.

1. _____ are people who have special knowledge.

2. _____ are buildings of any kind.

3. If an object is _____, it is strong and steady.

4. If you are _____, you reach your goal or get a good result.

B. **Choose the best option for each statement or question.**

1. A **tower** is normally _____.

   a. tall and thin

   b. short and round

2. A **designer** might work on a new _____.

   a. text message

   b. cell phone

3. An example of a **product** is _____.

   a. a box of spaghetti

   b. a trip to Italy

4. Which of these are you more likely to **plan**? _____

   a. A weekend activity

   b. A yard of tape

GETTING MEANING FROM CONTEXT

A writer may explain certain words or phrases in a text using a definition or a synonym (a word or phrase with a similar meaning). These often follow words such as *that is . . .* or *in other words . . .* or are set apart with parentheses, dashes, or commas. Definitions may also be provided below the text, as footnotes.

Refer to the passage on pages 25–26 to answer the questions below.

1. What does *by itself* mean in paragraph 1? Write another way to say it.

   _____

2. What synonym is given for *collaborate* in the passage? _____

3. How could you define *prototype*? Scan the passage and note a definition.

   _____

CRITICAL THINKING

1. Reflecting. Think about a team you are part of. Are you usually the expert, organizer, or experimenter?

   _____

   _____

   _____

2. Interpreting. What do you think Wujec means when he says, "Every project has its own marshmallow"?

   _____

   _____

   _____

EXPLORE MORE

Learn more about Tom Wujec. Visit his TED speaker profile at TED.com.
Share what you learn with your class.

BUILD A TOWER, BUILD A TEAM

TOM WUJEC Designer, TED speaker

Through the Marshmallow Challenge, Tom Wujec has learned a lot about how people work together.

Some teams have problems because they jockey for power. In other words, team members spend too much time deciding who is in charge. Some teams sketch lots of different ideas, but then run out of time and don't finish their towers. And other teams assemble a tower that looks good—just before it collapses under the marshmallow's weight.

---

sketch: *v.* to draw quickly

assemble: *v.* to build

collapse: *v.* to fall down

In this lesson, you are going to watch segments of Wujec's TED Talk. Use the information above about his challenge to answer these questions.

1. What do people do when they are "jockeying for power"?

   _____

2. Why do some teams not finish their towers?

   _____

3. What happens to some teams' towers when they put the marshmallow on top?

   _____

Tom Wujec's **idea worth spreading** is that the Marshmallow Challenge can be a fun and playful way to teach lessons about teamwork and design.

TEDTALKS

A CHALLENGING TASK

PREVIEWING

A. **Read the excerpt from Wujec's talk. Complete the excerpt with the correct words or phrases (a–d).**

a. orienting   **c.** assembling

b. talk about it   **d.** planning, organizing

❝ So, normally, most people begin by _____ themselves to the task. They _____,

                                     1   2

they figure out what it's going to look like; they jockey for power. Then they spend some

time _____, they sketch, and they lay out spaghetti. They spend the majority of

                     3

their time _____ the sticks into ever-growing structures. ❯❯

                            4

B. **Watch (▶) the first segment of the talk, and check your answers to Exercise A.**

GETTING THE MAIN IDEA

What is the most important idea in this segment of the TED Talk? Read the statements and choose the one that best describes the main idea.

a. Teams usually don't make very stable structures.

b. Teams usually fight with each other.

c. Teams usually spend too much time planning and testing their structure.

UNDERSTANDING KEY DETAILS

**Teams usually go through four steps when they do the Marshmallow Challenge.
Study the diagram and match each step with a description.**

_____ **a.** Teams assemble their towers.   _____ **c.** Teams sketch designs for the structure.

_____ **b.** Teams finish their towers.   _____ **d.** Teams try to understand the task.

0	Minutes	18
Orient **Plan**		**Build** **Ta-Da!**

CRITICAL THINKING

Inferring. Why do you think some teams "jockey for power"?

_____

_____

COLLABORATION IS KEY

PREVIEWING

In his TED Talk, Wujec reveals who builds the tallest towers. How do you think the people below do in the challenge? Work with a partner to match each group with a bar in the chart. Then check your answers as you watch (▶) the second segment of the talk.

_____ **a.** Lawyers

_____ **b.** Architects and engineers

_____ **c.** CEOs and executive admins

_____ **d.** Business school students

_____ **e.** Kindergartners

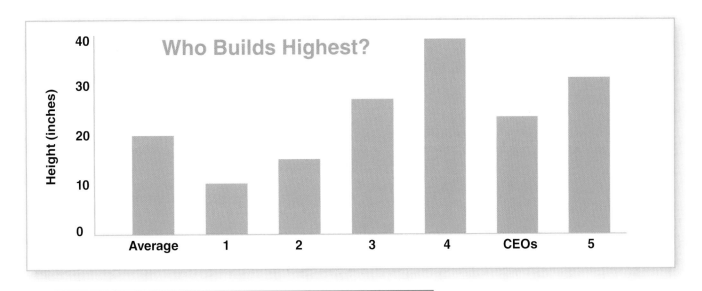

CEO: _n._ Chief Executive Officer; the person in charge of a business or organization

Executive Admin: _n._ a person who assists a CEO with administrative tasks

TEDTALKS

GETTING THE MAIN IDEA

Use information from Wujec's talk to answer each question.

1. According to Wujec, why do kindergarten students do well in the activity?

    a. They understand about strong structures.

    b. They don't fight with each other.

    c. They start with the marshmallow.

2. According to Wujec, it is better to build _____.

    a. very few prototypes.

    b. many prototypes.

    c. one good prototype.

SUMMARIZING

What do successful teams do when they build their towers? Check (✓) the best ideas from Wujec's talk.

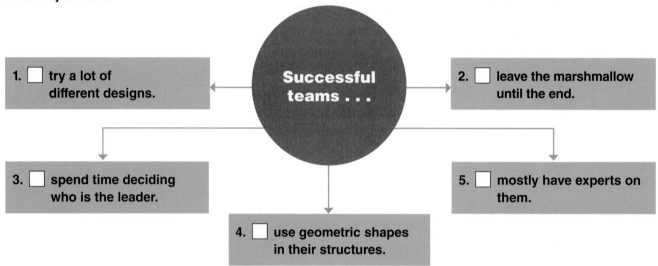

1. ☐ try a lot of different designs.

Successful teams . . .

2. ☐ leave the marshmallow until the end.

3. ☐ spend time deciding who is the leader.

4. ☐ use geometric shapes in their structures.

5. ☐ mostly have experts on them.

CRITICAL THINKING

1. Reflecting. How well do you think you and your classmates would do with the Marshmallow Challenge? Give reasons for your answer.

_____

_____

_____

2. Applying. What kind of structure do you think would work best in the Marshmallow Challenge? Work in groups and design the best structure on paper. If possible, try building it.

_____

_____

_____

EXPLORE MORE

Watch more of Tom Wujec's TED Talk at TED.com. What happens when Wujec adds a financial reward for the winning group? Why? Share what you learn with your class.

Project

A. **Work in a small team. You are going to design, perform, and share a team-building task.**

- Choose at least four everyday objects, such as the items below, to use in your task.

- Brainstorm ideas for a task using those objects.

- Choose one task idea, and decide the goal (for example, to build a bridge between two desks) and a time limit.

- Try the task as a team. Keep a note of your result.

- Demonstrate your task to other teams in your class, and have them try the task.

- Observe how the other teams perform the task and how their performance compares with your own team's.

B. **Discuss these questions with your class.**

1. What was easy about the exercise? What was difficult?

2. Were there any problems in your group? How did you solve them?

3. Which of the other teams was most successful in your task? Why do you think they were successful?

4. What did you learn about working in a team?

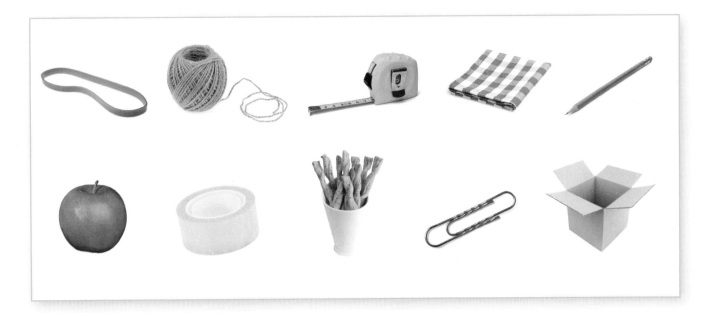

EXPLORE MORE

What else can we learn from a task using a marshmallow? Check out Joachim de Posada's TED Talk "Don't eat the marshmallow!" at TED.com. Discuss what you learn with your class.

OCEAN WONDERS

A sea fan fish swims among the coral reefs in the Caribbean Sea.

GOALS

IN THIS UNIT, YOU WILL:

- Read about a sea creature with a special ability.
- Learn about some amazing examples of ocean life.
- Explore how animals adapt to their environment.

THINK AND DISCUSS

1. What's the most amazing sea creature you can think of? What's special about it?

2. We've only explored about 3 percent of the world's oceans. Do you think it's important that we explore the other 97 percent? Why or why not?

PRE-READING

A. **Look at the photo and read the caption on page 39. Complete the statement below.**

This passage is mainly about ____.

a. problems with the world's coral reefs

b. the special ability of some sea animals

c. how some sea animals can move very fast

B. **Read the first two paragraphs of the passage quickly. Then answer the questions below.**

1. What kind of waters do cephalopods live in?

_____

_____

2. What are some examples of cephalopods?

_____

_____

3. What special abilities do these animals have?

_____

_____

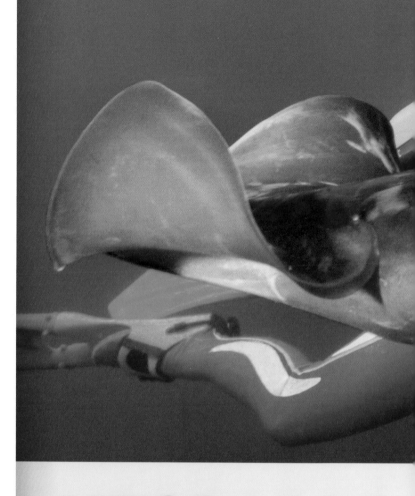

MESSAGES FROM THE SEA

Flashing colors, changing patterns, giant eyes . . . Meet the ocean's masters of disguise.

A female diver with a Humboldt squid in the Sea of Cortez, Mexico. The squid's skin can flash red and white when it senses danger.

1　In the warm, shallow waters of coral reefs live animals with an **amazing** ability. These animals, known as *cephalopods*, are able to change the appearance of their skin.

2　Squid, octopi, and cuttlefish are all types of cephalopods. Each of these animals has special cells under its **skin** that contain pigment, a colored **liquid**. A cephalopod can move these cells toward or away from its skin. This allows it to change the **pattern** and color of its appearance.

3　Cephalopods mainly use these cells as camouflage to hide from predators. For example, cephalopods can **blend in** to the color of the sea floor, making them invisible to predators. They can also change color to scare predators away. For example, the skin of the Caribbean reef squid is usually a plain brown. When a predator passes close by, the squid makes large "eye" patterns on its skin. This makes the squid appear much bigger than it really is. Squid can also use these cells to communicate other messages. When two male reef squid fight, black and white lines appear on their skin. These send a message that the squid is **fierce**. A reef squid **searching** for a mate can flash colorful patterns, sending a message that it is **attractive**.

4   Amazingly, reef squid can send two messages at the same time. They can send one message on their right side and a different message on their left side. For example, when males are searching for a mate, they flash attractive patterns on one side of their body. This is the side a female sees. On the other side of their bodies they can show their fierce zebra stripes. This is the side other males see. They can quickly flip the messages if the female swims to the other side!

5   With the ability to display 30 colors and patterns, the incredible Caribbean reef squid really is a master of disguise and a skillful communicator.

Caribbean reef squid live in the reefs of the Caribbean Sea.

---

shallow: *adj.* not deep

cell: *n.* a very small part that forms living things: e.g., a blood cell

camouflage: *n.* a way of hiding by making something look like its surroundings

predator: *n.* an animal that lives by killing and eating other animals

▼ Chromatophores are special cells that allow cephalopods to change the pattern and color of their skin.

A male reef squid with unusual skin patterns

Two Caribbean reef squid swim in the warm waters near the Netherlands Antilles.

Developing Reading Skills

GETTING THE MAIN IDEAS

Use information from the passage on pages 39–40 to answer each question.

1. Which sentence best describes the main idea of the passage?

    a. Cephalopods are some of the most attractive animals in the ocean.

    b. Cephalopods have an amazing ability to change the way they look.

    c. Cephalopods can communicate better than any other ocean animal.

2. What are two reasons that cephalopods change their skin color and pattern? Check (✔) the best phrases.

    ☐ **a.** To send messages to other animals

    ☐ **b.** To play games with each other

    ☐ **c.** To hide from dangerous predators

IDENTIFYING PURPOSE

Where in the passage can you find answers to the questions below? Match each question below with a paragraph (2–5).

a. What are cephalopods and what can they do? _____

b. What does the writer think about reef squid? _____

c. For what purposes do cephalopods mainly use their special skin cells? _____

d. How can a reef squid send more than one message? _____

IDENTIFYING REFERENTS

Writers often use words like *it*, *them*, and *they* to refer back to someone or something that was introduced earlier. Paying attention to these words will help you better understand how ideas are connected.

The sentences below come from the passage. Read each sentence and look at the underlined word. Find the word or words that it refers to and write them on the line.

1. A cephalopod can move these cells toward or away from its skin. This allows <u>it</u> to change the pattern and color of its appearance. _____

2. For example, cephalopods can blend in to the color of the sea floor, making <u>them</u> invisible to predators. _____

3. This makes the squid appear much bigger than <u>it</u> really is. _____

4. Amazingly, reef squid can send two messages at the same time. <u>They</u> can send one message on their right side and a different message on their left side. _____

5. For example, when males are searching for a mate, <u>they</u> flash attractive patterns on one side of their body. _____

BUILDING VOCABULARY

A. **Correct each sentence by replacing the bold word with another bold word from the passage.**

1. Something that is **fierce** causes great wonder or surprise. _____

2. If an animal is **attractive**, it is aggressive and sometimes violent. _____

3. The outer layer of the body of a person or an animal is called the **pattern**. _____

4. Water and ink are two kinds of **skin**. _____

5. If you are **blending in**, you are looking for something. _____

B. **Use bold words from the passage on pages 39–40 to complete this paragraph.**

Cephalopods can change the color and pattern of their _____. They use special
                                                        1
cells that contain colored _____, or pigment. For example, male squid that are
                           2
fighting change their pattern to show that they are _____. A squid that is
                                                    3
_____ for a mate makes its skin more attractive. By changing the way it looks, a
4
squid can send many messages. With such a special skill, cephalopods are truly

_____ creatures.
5

GETTING MEANING FROM CONTEXT

A. **The prefix *in-* can mean "not." Scan the passage to find two words with *in-*. Use the context to write a definition for each one. Check your ideas with a dictionary.**

1. [Paragraph 3] *in_____*   Meaning: _____

2. [Paragraph 5] *in_____*   Meaning: _____

B. **Read the information. Use the context to match each bold word with a definition.**

You might think we have explored everywhere on Earth, but that is **incorrect**. Even today, our knowledge of the oceans is **incomplete**. In fact, we have only explored a small part of the undersea world. We are also learning more about the animals that live underwater. Scientists have discovered that a jellyfish, for example, is **incapable** of thinking for itself, as it has no brain.

1. Wrong; not true   _____

2. Not able to do something   _____

3. Not including everything   _____

CRITICAL THINKING

1. Inferring. In paragraph 5, the writer refers to the reef squid as a "master of disguise." What do you think this means? How else could you say this?

_____

_____

2. Evaluating. The Caribbean reef squid can change its appearance in many different ways. Which one do you think is most useful? Give reasons for your answer.

_____

_____

EXPLORE MORE

Learn more about amazing sea animals. Visit nationalgeographic.com/ocean/photos/unique-sea-creatures. Choose one of the animals, and tell a partner about it.

▶ A flying gurnard fish spreads its colorful "wings" to scare away predators.

TEDTALKS

UNDERWATER ASTONISHMENTS

DAVID GALLO Oceanographer, TED speaker

David Gallo is an ocean scientist at the Woods Hole Oceanographic Institute (WHOI) in Massachusetts, U.S.A.

Gallo has spent many years studying the geography of the deepest ocean and the surprising creatures that live there. Now he and other scientists at WHOI are also learning about the animals that live in shallow water. Some of them have a special ability—they can change their color and pattern to send messages. They can also hide from predators by looking like the sand, rocks, and plants that surround them. As Gallo says, "That's an amazing thing."

---

geography: *n.* the natural features (such as rivers, mountains, etc.) of a place

In this lesson, you are going to watch Gallo's TED Talk. Use the information above about Gallo to answer the questions.

1. Where does David Gallo work?

   _____

2. What kind of animals are the scientists studying?

   _____

3. What "amazing thing" have scientists learned about these animals?

   _____

   _____

Gallo's **idea worth spreading** is that we still have much to learn about our home planet— especially our oceans, where 97 percent of what's out there remains unexplored.

Delicate skin patterns on a giant cuttlefish.

PREVIEWING

A. **Scan the following excerpt from Gallo's TED Talk. What animal is he talking about? What can it do? Discuss with a partner.**

❝ I want to jump up to shallow water now and look at some creatures that are positively amazing. [. . .] It's just fascinating how cephalopods can, with their incredible eyes, sense their surroundings, look at light, look at patterns. Here's an octopus moving across the reef. [It] finds a spot to settle down, curls up, and then disappears into the background. Tough thing to do. ❞

settle down: *v.* to sit comfortably   **curl up:** *v.* to lie in a curved position

B. **What can we infer from this excerpt? Check (✓) two true statements.**

☐ **1.** This animal cannot see very well.

☐ **2.** This animal is good at hiding.

☐ **3.** This animal can be found near reefs.

GETTING THE MAIN IDEAS

A. Watch (▶) the segment from Gallo's TED Talk, and check your answers on page 46.

B. What two ideas does Gallo mention in this segment of his talk?

1. Cephalopods are amazing because they can change the way they look.

2. The number of cephalopods that live in shallow ocean waters is declining.

3. Cephalopods change their appearance because there are many predators around them.

UNDERSTANDING KEY DETAILS

Read the sentences about Gallo's "underwater astonishments." Complete each sentence as you watch (▶) his TED Talk again.

1. Octopi _____ so they can match them.

    a. look at their surroundings

    b. swim quickly over reefs

    c. move like ocean waves

2. Cuttlefish can _____.

    a. make their tentacles look like undersea plants

    b. make their eyes look much smaller

    c. make their bodies look bigger

3. When cephalopods are fighting, they _____.

    a. sometimes kill each other

    b. usually don't hurt each other

    c. often hurt each other

4. If an octopus is surprised by a predator, it _____.

    a. attacks the predator

    b. hides under a rock

    c. makes itself look big

RECOGNIZING THE SPEAKER'S TONE AND MESSAGE

Read this excerpt from Gallo's talk, and answer the questions below.

❝ In the next bit, we're going to see a couple [of] squid. . . . Now males, when they fight, if they're really aggressive, they turn white. . . . Now, here's a male on the left and a female on the right, and the male has managed to split his coloration so the female only always sees the kinder gentler squid in him. . . . Let's take a look at it again. Watch the coloration: white on the right, brown on the left. He takes a step back—so he's keeping off the other males by splitting his body—and comes up on the other side. . . . Bingo! Now I'm told that's not just a squid phenomenon with males, but I don't know." [Laughter] ❞

1. Which statement best matches Gallo's message in this segment?

    a. Male squid are surprisingly aggressive creatures.

    b. Male squid use color to show different sides of their character.

    c. Male squid have more attractive coloring than female squid.

2. Why do you think the audience laughs when Gallo talks about male squid changing their colors? What point does he make?

_____

_____

_____

SYNTHESIZING INFORMATION

What have you learned about cephalopods? Work with a partner to complete the Venn diagram using the information below.

a. can make tentacles look like plants

b. can change skin to look like a rock

c. can change patterns on skin when fighting

d. can change skin to blend into background

e. can make large "eye" pattern on skin

f. can change pattern and color of skin

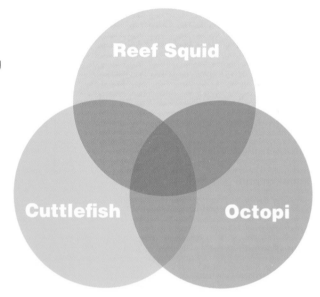

CRITICAL THINKING

1. Questioning. What else would you like to know about cephalopods? Write two or three questions that you could ask David Gallo. Share them with a partner.

_____

_____

2. Reflecting. How do humans disguise themselves or change their appearance? What messages do the clothes you wear send to other people?

_____

_____

EXPLORE MORE

Watch David Gallo's full TED talk at TED.com. What other types of animals does he talk about? Share what you learn with your class.

A pygmy seahorse swims in the warm waters of the Philippines.

A. **Work in teams of four or five. You are going to research animals that have extraordinary abilities.**

- Research one of these animals: pygmy seahorse, stick insect, arctic fox.
- Collect information about what kind of animal it is. For example, where it lives, what it eats, and what preys on it.
- Prepare a presentation. Think about how David Gallo presents his information—for example, by describing what is happening as the audience watches a video.

B. **Give your presentation. Follow these guidelines:**

- Your presentation should last about five minutes. Include time for your classmates to ask questions.
- Be sure everyone in your team has a job to do during the presentation. Some jobs include: speaking during the presentation, operating the slides and video, keeping time, or answering questions from the audience.

C. **Discuss the following questions with your class.**

1. Where did you find information about your animal?
2. How many sources of information did you use?
3. What was difficult about the project? What was easy?
4. How did you decide who would do the different jobs?

EXPLORE MORE

David Gallo mentions oceanographer and inventor Edith Widder in his TED Talk. Find out more about Widder's discoveries at TED.com. What creatures does Widder find amazing, and why? What does she say about the need for additional ocean exploration?

WHAT WE WEAR

GOALS

IN THIS UNIT, YOU WILL:

- Read about how clothes affect our feelings about ourselves.
- Learn how a fashion expert chooses clothes.
- Explore different kinds of uniforms.

THINK AND DISCUSS

1. How do you decide what clothes to wear to work, to school, and at home?

2. Do you think our clothes affect how people see us? Give reasons for your answer.

A woman dressed in a colorful costume for the Burning Man Festival in Nevada, U.S.A.

PRE-READING

A. **Look at the photo and read the caption on page 53.**

What is the article about?

a. How people choose the clothes they wear

b. How people dress for their jobs

c. How people's clothes make them feel

B. **Look at the title of the passage and quickly read the first three paragraphs (pages 53–54). Then answer the questions below.**

1. What do you think paragraph 2 is mostly about?

   a. A description of an experiment

   b. The opinions of a blogger

   c. A biography of two scientists

2. What do you think paragraph 3 is mostly about?

   a. Why people wear uniforms

   b. How special clothes can change people's behavior

   c. Why it is important to have a dress-code for certain jobs

THE SCIENCE OF STYLE

A couple look at clothes in a store. Researchers are looking at how clothes affect our feelings.

1 Deciding what to wear in the morning is a challenge for some people. We often worry about what others will think of us because of our clothes. But researchers are beginning to think that our clothing has an equally powerful effect on how we see ourselves.

2 Scientists Adam Galinsky and Hajo Adams report that there is science behind our **style**. In their research, Galinsky and Adams had some participants wear white lab coats similar to the ones scientists or doctors wear. Other participants wore their normal clothes. The participants took a test that measured their ability to **pay attention**. The people wearing the white coats **performed** better than the people in regular clothes.

3 Galinsky and Adams think that the white coats made the participants feel more confident and careful. The researchers also believe that other kinds of "symbolic" clothes can influence the **behavior** of the people wearing them. A police officer's **uniform** or a judge's robe, for example, increase the wearer's feeling of power or confidence. And in workplaces that have a dress code, "symbolic" clothes may also affect how well employees do their jobs.

4 Fashion blogger Jessica Quirk believes that our clothes greatly affect how we feel about ourselves. According to Quirk, "There is joy and **luck** and confidence in what we wear." On her blog called "What I Wore," Quirk posts a photo of what she's wearing every day. She says that people should pay more attention to what they wear. For example, we should choose a look that makes us feel more **creative** and happy. One way to do this at work is to "dress up for the exciting job we want," she says, "not the boring job we have." Another way is to wear special clothes that mean something to us. For example, Quirk wears one pair of shoes to all her important meetings. They are her "lucky" shoes.

5 As Quirk **points out**—and as researchers have discovered—our clothes are "like our second skin." The clothes we wear can affect

Jessica Quirk

our behavior. They can also tell the world something about us, without us having to say a word.

---

symbolic: *adj.* representing something

influence: *v.* to affect people or things

dress code: *n.* a set of rules for what you can wear

look: *n.* a style or fashion

NOW PAY ATTENTION!

In Galinsky and Adams's experiment, participants saw cards with different-colored words on them. Participants had to say the color of the word they saw, not the word itself.

The people wearing the lab coats said the correct color of the word more often. The researchers believe that wearing lab coats made participants pay more attention to the test. Their behavior was, in fact, more like that of a doctor or a scientist.

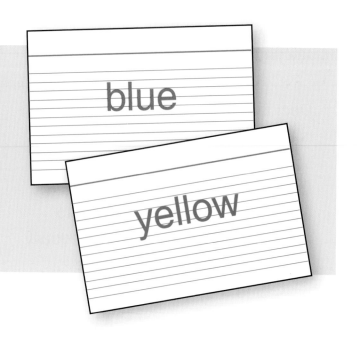

GETTING THE MAIN IDEAS

Use information from the passage on pages 53–54 to answer each question.

1. What is the main idea of the passage? Complete the sentence.

   The clothes we wear _____

   a. can affect how we feel

   b. should be symbolic

   c. make us feel more powerful

2. What are some examples of symbolic clothes the writer mentions? What effects can they have on the wearer?

   _____

   _____

MAKING CONNECTIONS

Writers often use words and phrases such as *believes that, says that, reported that,* and *thinks that* to show what someone says or thinks.

A. **Underline the phrases in the passage on pages 53–54 that link a person / people with what they say or believe.**

B. **According to the passage, who says or reports the following statements? Write the letters of each statement (a–d) in the Venn diagram.**

> **a.** There is science behind our style.
>
> **b.** Symbolic clothes influence how people work.
>
> **c.** Our clothes are like a second skin.
>
> **d.** People should pay more attention to what they wear.

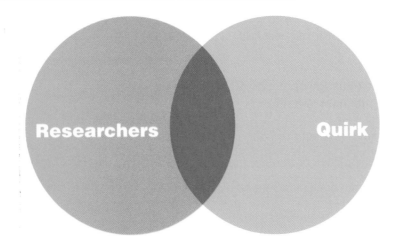

Researchers   Quirk

UNDERSTANDING A PROCESS

What happened in Galinsky and Adams's experiment? Put the steps into the correct order by writing 1–4. Then add a sequence word to each step.

First   ~~Next~~   Finally   Then

____ a. _Next_____ participants looked at words each written in a different color.

____ b. _____ the researchers counted the correct items.

____ c. _____ the participants said the colors, not the words.

_1_ d. _____ the researchers gave some participants white coats to wear.

BUILDING VOCABULARY

A. Find the bold words in the passage on pages 53–54. Then complete the sentences with the correct words.

1. Your personal _____ is the way you dress.

2. Quirk thinks people need to _____ to what they wear.

3. A person's _____ is the things that he or she does.

4. Some workers, like nurses and waiters, wear a _____ to work.

B. Match each word to its definition.

1. creative ____   a. to do an action or activity

2. perform ____   b. chance, fortune

3. points out ____   c. draw someone's attention to important information

4. luck ____   d. showing an ability to think of new ideas

GETTING MEANING FROM CONTEXT

Many words can be used as two or more parts of speech (e.g., noun, verb). Each part of speech can have a different meaning.

Read the sentences taken from the passage on pages 53–54. Write the part of speech of the underlined word. Then check (✓) the best definition.

_____ 1. Quirk <u>posts</u> a photo of what she's wearing every day.

☐ a. Long, standing pieces of wood or metal

☐ b. To put messages or signs where others can see them

2. Scientists Adam Galinsky and Hajo Adams <u>report</u> that there is science behind our style

☐ **a.** To tell people about a piece of research

☐ **b.** A written or spoken description of a situation or an event

3. The participants took a <u>test</u> that measured their ability to pay attention

☐ **a.** To use a problem that measures a person's knowledge or abilities

☐ **b.** A problem that measures a person's knowledge or abilities

4. A police officer's <u>uniform</u> can increase the wearer's feeling of power or confidence

☐ **a.** A special kind of clothing that is worn by everyone in a group or an organization

☐ **b.** Staying the same at all times, in all places

CRITICAL THINKING

1. Inferring. Why do you think wearing a white lab coat made participants more confident and careful?

_____

_____

_____

2. Applying. What other experiment might the researchers have used to test how closely people pay attention?

_____

_____

_____

EXPLORE MORE

Watch Jessica Quirk's TED Talk at TED.com. Choose one of her outfits that you like the best. Tell your class and say why you like the outfit.

Four women pose in the fashionable Harajuku District of Tokyo, Japan.

TEDTALKS

WEARING NOTHING NEW

JESSI ARRINGTON Designer, TED speaker

🔊 Jessi Arrington describes herself as "outfit obsessed."

She says that her favorite color is "rainbow," and her outfits include many different colors and patterns. Arrington has a lot of clothes, but she doesn't spend a lot of money on them. She buys them in secondhand stores. For her trip to the TED conference, Arrington brought nothing but a tiny suitcase full of underwear. She then spent every day of the conference shopping for a new outfit.

---

outfit: *n.* a set of clothes worn for a special event

obsessed: *adj.* very interested in something

secondhand: *adj.* not new, used before by someone else

In this lesson, you are going to watch segments of Arrington's TED Talk. Use the information about her above to answer the questions.

1. What color does Arrington like most?

    _____

2. Where does Arrington shop for clothing?

    _____

3. What did Arrington bring to the TED conference?

    _____

Arrington's **idea worth spreading** is that secondhand shopping can reduce our impact on the environment and our wallets, while still being fun and creative.

PART 1

A PERSONAL TREASURE HUNT

PREVIEWING

A. Scan the following excerpt from Arrington's TED Talk. How does Arrington describe herself in her secondhand clothes? Underline the answer.

« Secondhand shopping allows me to reduce the impact my wardrobe has on the environment and on my wallet. I get to meet all kinds of great people; my dollars usually go to a good cause; I look pretty unique; and it makes shopping like my own personal treasure hunt. »

B. Read the excerpt again. Why does she like shopping at secondhand stores? Compare your answer with a partner.

---

wardrobe: *n.* all of the clothes that a person owns

good cause: *n.* a charity, a way to give money to help people who are in need

unique: *adj.* unusual or special in some way

GETTING THE MAIN IDEAS

Watch (▶) the first segment of Arrington's TED Talk. What is the purpose of this segment of her talk? Choose the two best statements.

a. To show what's in her suitcase

b. To describe how she shops for clothes

c. To explain that she loves clothes

d. To point out that she is poor

UNDERSTANDING DETAILS

How does Jessi Arrington decide what clothes to buy? Check (✓) the questions she asks when she is shopping.

_____ **1.** Does it fit me?

_____ **2.** Is it a designer brand?

_____ **3.** Do I need it?

_____ **4.** Do I like the color?

_____ **5.** Is the price less than $20?

CRITICAL THINKING

1. Interpreting. Arrington says she is going to "make a very public confession." Why does she say this?

_____

2. Reflecting. Do you shop for clothes in the same way as Arrington? Why or why not?

_____

A WEEK OF OUTFITS

UNDERSTANDING KEY DETAILS

Read these statements describing what Arrington learned during her "wearing nothing new." Work with a partner to guess what the missing word is for each sentence. Then check your ideas as you watch (▶) this segment of her TED Talk.

1. Wearing _____ colors can make you feel happy.

2. It isn't important to _____ and act like other people.

3. If you are _____, you can look good in anything.

4. People like to _____ to you when you wear interesting clothes.

RECOGNIZING THE SPEAKER'S POINT OF VIEW

Read the excerpt from Jessi Arrington's TED Talk, and answer the questions on the next page.

> ❝ Confidence is key. If you think you look good in something, you almost certainly do. And if you don't think you look good in something, you're also probably right. [. . .] If you believe you're a beautiful person inside and out, there is no look that you can't pull off. So there is no excuse for any of us here in this audience. ❞

---

key: *adj.* very important   **excuse:** *n.* a reason given for a mistake or a problem

1. Which statement best matches Arrington's opinion about dressing confidently?

   a. We should all dress in an unusual way.

   b. We should all believe that we are beautiful.

   c. We should make sure we look good in our clothes.

2. What do you think Arrington means by ". . . there is no look that you can't pull off"?

COMPARING MESSAGES

Read the quotes below from this unit. Then answer the questions.

A. Jessi Arrington

" Fitting in is way overrated. Just be who you are. If you are surrounding yourself with the right people, they will not only get it, they will appreciate it. "

B. Jessica Quirk

" Dressing for the job you want rather than the job you have can give you a day full of confidence. "

1. Match the summary sentences below to quotes A and B.

   _____ 1. It is important to dress in a way that helps you work well.

   _____ 2. It is important to dress in a way that shows your personality and style.

2. Discuss these questions with your partner. Give reasons for your answers.

   a. When do you think it is important to dress in a way that makes you happy?

   b. Do you think you can wear clothes that make you happy *and* that help you work well? Explain your answer.

CRITICAL THINKING

1. Interpreting. Why is Jessi Arrington trying to learn to "let go" of her clothes?

2. Reflecting. What do you think the clothes you're wearing today say about you?

EXPLORE MORE

Go online and search for secondhand stores. Share pictures of clothing you think are distinctive or would suit you.

Project

A firefighter putting out a fire in California, U.S.A.

A. **Work with a partner. You are going to research uniforms and other "symbolic" clothing.**

- Choose three people you know who wear uniforms. For example, a student, a firefighter, or a bus driver.
- Prepare three or more questions to ask each person about their uniform. You could ask them what parts of the uniform mean, how they feel when wearing the uniform, or what they would change about it.
- Prepare a poster session that gives facts about the people you researched.

B. **Hold the poster session. Follow these guidelines:**

- One member of your team should be at your poster to answer questions. Take turns circulating and staying with the poster.
- When you are looking at your classmates' posters, ask at least one question for each team.

C. **Discuss these questions with your class.**

1. What was the most surprising fact you discovered?
2. Was it difficult to find the information you needed?
3. What else would you like to know about uniforms and their meanings?

EXPLORE MORE

Go to photography.nationalgeographic.com and click on the "People and Culture" link. Find a photograph of someone wearing an unusual outfit. Share it with your class.

MOMENTS AND MEMORIES

GOALS

IN THIS UNIT, YOU WILL:

- Read about a place that stores millions of memories.
- Learn how one man is recording his memories.
- Explore other people's memories.

THINK AND DISCUSS

1. How often do you take photos or shoot video? What events do you record?

2. Would you want to remember every day of your life? Why or why not?

A 1917 camping party on top of a fallen sequoia
tree in California, U.S.A.

PRE-READING

A. Look at the title and headings on pages 66–67. Complete the statement.

This passage is mainly about _____.

a. a family's photos

b. how old photos help us to remember the past

c. the story of an old photographer

B. Read the first paragraph and choose the correct answer for each question below.

1. What do people worldwide do about 6 billion times every month?

   a. Send photos to their friends

   b. Post photos on the Internet

   c. Watch videos on the Internet

2. According to the writer, we sometimes forget that photographs are _____.

   a. expensive

   b. common

   c. special

A photographer processes film among icebergs in Alaska, U.S.A., 1910.

1   Every month, people worldwide upload about 6 billion photos to the Internet. Photography is now so common, it is easy to forget that photographs—and the memories they hold—can be very **precious**.

MEMORY ARCHIVE

2   In a cold, windowless basement in Washington D.C., there is a man who knows the real value of a photograph. Since 1983, Bill Bonner has **looked after** *National Geographic's* photo archive. The archive holds around 8 million prints—many over 100 years old.

PRESERVING THE PAST

3   In his long career, Bonner has looked at hundreds of thousands of photos. He believes each **image** holds a memory. Some of the pictures **record** moments in history. Many others, he says, show "people like us, just doing our thing, living our life." Many of these memories have been forgotten by the outside world. But they still have the power to tell us a lot about the past.

IMAGES FROM THE PAST

4   When the archive's earliest photos were taken, photography was difficult and expensive. Photographers needed special **equipment** and chemicals to develop their pictures. **Cameras** were large and heavy—some weighed 20 pounds (9 kilos) or more. Early explorers used these massive cameras to photograph people

and places that most people had never seen. Photography expeditions took several months, or even years. "They dedicated their lives to this," Bonner says.

5   Bonner feels **responsible** for keeping these memories alive, for people now and in the future. Many of the images are fragile, and he has to be very careful to **preserve** them. For Bonner, these figures from the distant past are almost like his ancestors. "For me," he says, "it's like opening your grandparents' family album for the first time."

---

archive: *n.* a place that stores historical material

develop: *v.* to make a photograph using a special process

ancestor: *n.* someone related to you who lived in the past

dedicated: *v.* to give something your complete effort

DIGITAL PHOTOS TAKEN BY AMERICANS

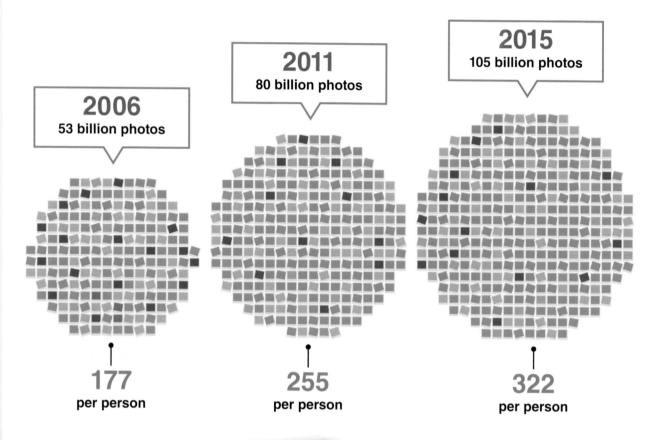

2006
53 billion photos

2011
80 billion photos

2015
105 billion photos

177
per person

255
per person

322
per person

Just under half of all digital photos in the United States
are taken with smartphones.

Image-Obsessed

Surveys show an explosion in the number
of photos Americans have taken since
2006. The movement from film to digital
means that consumers are less worried
about cost and can be more creative.
What's the downside? Sorting and
keeping track of all those digital files. And,
with fewer people printing their photos,
storing images in a safe place is critical.

Source: NGM, Infotrends

Newspaper boys cool off in a New York City park fountain, 1916.

Developing Reading Skills

GETTING THE MAIN IDEAS

Use information from the passage on pages 66–67 to answer each question.

1. What is the main idea of the passage? Complete the sentence below.

    The photos in the *National Geographic* archive ____.

    a. keep Bill Bonner very busy

    b. are kept in a cold basement

    c. tell us stories about the past

2. Why are the archive's photos special to Bill Bonner? Check (✔) two reasons.

    ☐ a. They show ordinary people doing ordinary things.

    ☐ b. They are mostly black-and-white images.

    ☐ c. They are the work of dedicated photographers.

IDENTIFYING APPROXIMATE NUMBERS

Writers use approximate numbers (*about 3 million years ago, nearly a month long*) if the exact number is not known or not important. These words signal that a number is approximate: *about, almost, approximately, around, nearly, (just) over / under.*

Look back at the reading passage on pages 66–67 and underline the approximate numbers and circle the signal words. Then answer the questions below.

1. How many photos are put on the Internet every month?

    _____

2. How many photos are in the archive?

    _____

3. How old are some photos in the archive?

    _____

4. How much did some early cameras weigh?

    _____

69

UNDERSTANDING VISUALS

Look at the infographic and text about digital photographs on page 68. Then answer the questions by writing *T* for True or *F* for False. Correct the false statements.

_____ **1.** The number of digital photos taken by Americans has decreased since 2006.

_____ **2.** In 2011, Americans took approximately 80 million photos.

_____ **3.** In 2006, Americans took an average of 177 photos per person.

_____ **4.** In the U.S.A., over half of digital photos are taken using a smartphone.

_____ **5.** People tend to be less worried about the cost of digital photography.

BUILDING VOCABULARY

A. **Choose the correct words to complete the sentences.**

Looking at an old **image / equipment** lets us visit a world that has disappeared. Early explorers took heavy **camera / equipment** with them to **record / look after** people and places that other people had not seen. Now these photographs are **recorded / preserved** by archivists such as Bill Bonner.

B. **Complete the sentences with the correct word or phrase. One item is extra.**

cameras	look after	precious	records	responsible

1. Photographs from the early 19th century are _____. Not many photos survive from that time.

2. A photo _____ a memory of a person, a place, or an event.

3. Photo archivists _____ old images. These images are often kept in environmentally controlled rooms so the photos aren't damaged.

4. The first _____ were large, heavy, and expensive.

GETTING MEANING FROM CONTEXT

1. Bonner thinks the archive's photos have been forgotten by "the outside world." What does that phrase mean? How else could you express this idea?

_____

2. The writer says that "Many of the images are *fragile*, and [Bonner] has to be very careful to preserve them." What does *fragile* mean?

_____

CRITICAL THINKING

1. Inferring. Bill Bonner says that looking at the photos in the archive is "like opening your grandparents' family album for the first time." What do you think he means?

    _____

    _____

    _____

2. Reflecting. Think about the photos you take. What kinds of photos would you preserve for future generations?

    _____

    _____

    _____

EXPLORE MORE

Look at images from the archive at photography.nationalgeographic.com. Choose an image that you think is interesting, and tell your class about it. Give reasons for your choice.

Bill Bonner, archivist at *National Geographic*, at work.

TEDTALKS

ONE SECOND EVERY DAY

CESAR KURIYAMA Video maker, TED speaker

Cesar Kuriyama had a successful career in advertising but found the job draining. Kuriyama's life changed when he saw a TED Talk by Stefan Sagmeister called "The Power of Time Off."

Sagmeister spoke about how he takes a year off work every seven years so he can do his own projects. Kuriyama was inspired and thought "I have to do that." So, at age 30, Kuriyama quit his job and started a number of projects. One of these projects is called "One Second Every Day." Each day, he films and compiles one second of his life. He hopes that this visualization will help trigger more memories when he is older.

---

advertising: *n.* the business of creating advertisements and commercials that sell products

draining: *adj.* making someone feel very tired

visualization: *n.* a mental picture

trigger: *v.* to cause something to happen or exist

In this lesson, you are going to watch segments of Kuriyama's TED Talk. Read the information about Kuriyama above, and then answer the questions.

1. Why was Kuriyama unhappy in his job?

   _____

2. What inspired Kuriyama to quit his job?

   _____

3. What is the "One Second Every Day" project?

   _____

   _____

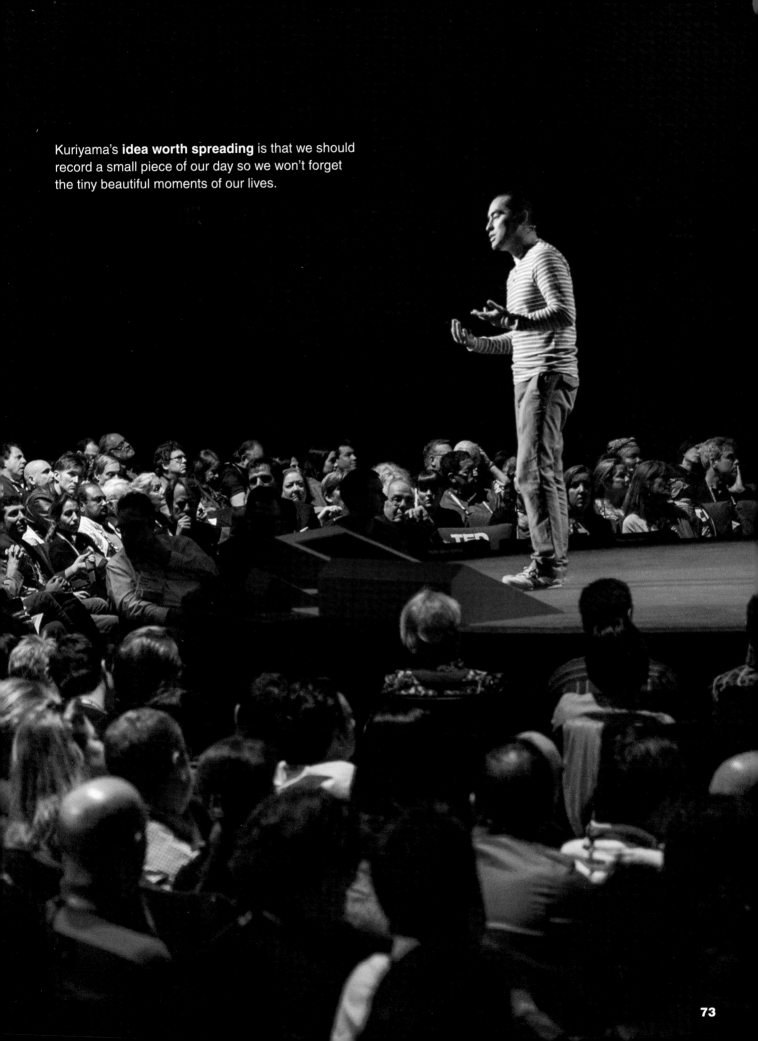

Kuriyama's **idea worth spreading** is that we should record a small piece of our day so we won't forget the tiny beautiful moments of our lives.

WHY "ONE SECOND EVERY DAY"?

PREVIEWING

Scan the following extract from Kuriyama's TED Talk. Why did he start the "One Second Every Day" project? Share your ideas with a partner.

> ❝ The purpose of this project is . . . I hate not remembering things that I've done in the past. There's all these things that I've done with my life that I have no recollection of unless someone brings it up, and sometimes I think, 'Oh yeah, that's something that I did.' ❯❯

recollection: *n.* the act of remembering

GETTING THE MAIN IDEAS

A. Watch (▶) the first segment of Kuriyama's TED Talk. What mistake did Kuriyama make when he first started his project? What inspired him to avoid making that mistake again?

_____

_____

B. Check (✔) the three main ideas of this segment of Kuriyama's TED Talk.

☐ **1.** Seeing an image from the past helps you remember.

☐ **2.** It is ideal to use the latest technology to keep your memories.

☐ **3.** Recording your life inspires you to do something interesting every day.

☐ **4.** Recording your life can help make you famous on the Internet.

☐ **5.** Editing a video down to one second helps you remember more.

CRITICAL THINKING

1. Interpreting. What does Kuriyama mean when he says, "Time just seems to start blurring and blending into each other"?

_____

_____

2. Synthesizing. In Unit 1, Matt Cutts suggests trying a different project every 30 days to achieve change. Cesar Kuriyama decided to do one project and continue it for the rest of his life. Which appeals to you more? Which would be easier to do?

_____

_____

PART 2

GOOD DAYS AND BAD DAYS

RECOGNIZING THE SPEAKER'S MESSAGE

A. **Read the excerpt from the next segment of Kuriyama's TED Talk. Underline the sentences that best state his message in this part of the talk. Then write a sentence that expresses his message in your own words.**

❝ We tend to take our cameras out when we're doing awesome things. Or we're, "Oh, yeah, this party, let me take a picture." But we rarely do that when we're having a bad day, and something horrible is happening. And I found that it's actually been very, very important to record even just that one second of a really bad moment. It really helps you appreciate the good times. It's not always a good day, so when you have a bad one, I think it's important to remember it, just as much as it is important to remember the [good] days. ❯❯

_____

appreciate: _v._ to be thankful for

_____

_____

B. **Now watch (▶) the next segment of Kuriyama's TED Talk, and answer the questions.**

1. What was the bad event that changed the "One Second Every Day" project?

_____

_____

2. Why did Kuriyama decide not to include himself in the videos?

_____

_____

_____

UNDERSTANDING KEY DETAILS

Read these sentences describing Kuriyama's TED Talk. Write T for *True* or F for *False* as you watch the TED Talk again.

_____ **1.** Kuriyama wanted to spend more time with his family during his year off.

_____ **2.** When his family member was ill, Kuriyama spent a lot of time at the hospital.

_____ **3.** Kuriyama says people should use special equipment to record their lives.

_____ **4.** Kuriyama thinks it is unwise for people to share their videos online.

_____ **5.** Some of the clips have Kuriyama in them.

CRITICAL THINKING

1. Evaluating. Read the quote from the last part of Kuriyama's talk. Do you think everyone would benefit from having one second to remember every day? Why or why not?

    ❝ I think it would be interesting to see what everyone did with a project like this. I think everyone would have a different interpretation of it. I think everyone would benefit from just having that one second to remember every day. Personally, I'm tired of forgetting, and this is a really easy thing to do. ❞

    _____

    interpretation: *n.* the way you understand something

    _____

    _____

2. Reflecting. Think of the last few days in your own life. Which second from each day would you choose to help you remember that day? Why? What were you doing?

    _____

    _____

    _____

    _____

EXPLORE MORE

Watch Kuriyama's complete TED Talk at TED.com. Which of the one-second clips he shows surprised you the most? Share your ideas with your class.

Project

A. **Work in a small group. You are going to plan a class media show about your memories.**

1. Find (or take) photos of an ordinary day in your life or the life of someone you know. Or, take one-second videos.

2. Bring the photos or videos to class.

3. Create some guidelines for the show using the following questions:

   - What is the purpose of the show?
   - How are you going to display the media?
   - What title will you give to the show?
   - How do you want viewers to feel when they see the videos and/or photos?

B. **Set up the show in your classroom. Look at all of your classmates' shows. Then share how they make you feel. Give reasons for your answers.**

1. Which images made you laugh?

2. Which ones made you sad?

3. Which ones had the strongest impact on you?

EXPLORE MORE

Go to TED.com and watch a TED Talk called "Capturing Memories in Video Art" by Gabriel Barcia-Colombo. How does Barcia-Colombo's work make you feel? Share your ideas with your class.

House H, a residential project
in Tokyo, designed by the
Japanese architect Sou Fujimoto.
Photograph by Iwan Baan.

BUILDING
SOLUTIONS

GOALS

IN THIS UNIT, YOU WILL:

- Read about unusual buildings.
- Learn about a city built on water.
- Explore some unusual structures around the world.

THINK AND DISCUSS

1. How would you describe a typical home in your town or city? For example, what materials is it made from?

2. What makes a neighborhood a nice place to live?

PRE-READING

A. Look at the photos and infographic, and read the captions on pages 80–83. Match each one with a description (a–c).

_____ Photo on page 80–81

_____ Infographic on page 82

_____ Photo on page 83

> a. An underground skyscraper
>
> b. An office building that people live in
>
> c. A home made from things that people threw away

B. What words would you use to describe each building? Discuss your ideas with a partner.

C. Who does the writer mention in the passage? Scan the passage on pages 80–82 for people's names and occupations, and complete the information below. Then read the whole passage to check your answers.

Name: Iwan Baan

Occupation: _____

Name: _____

Occupation: _____

Name: _____

Occupation: _____

People gather outside a store in Torre David, an abandoned office block in Caracas, Venezuela that residents turned into apartments. Photograph by Iwan Baan.

LIVING SPACES

In many **communities** around the world, people are finding creative ways to make the most of their resources.

resources: _n._ useful things that people, countries, or regions have

CITY IN A TOWER

1 The Torre David in Caracas, Venezuela, was designed to be a modern office building. But the project was abandoned when the **construction** company closed, and the building was never finished. However, local **residents** saw an opportunity. They began to turn the empty offices into apartments and stores. They painted the entrance and planted trees. As there were no working elevators, residents used taxis to reach the upper floors via the parking garage.

2 Within a few years, 3,000 people were sharing a community that they built themselves. The abandoned tower, says photographer and TED speaker Iwan Baan, turned into "a living city."

RECYCLED HOMES

3 In Huntsville, Texas, a community is building houses from recycled building **materials**. How did this start? Local builder and TED speaker Dan Phillips noticed that construction companies traditionally threw away large amounts of unused bricks, wood, and cement when they built homes. Phillips decided to work with local people and homeowners to build houses using these materials. These people are not **professional** builders, so Phillips teaches them the skills and **techniques** they need. The houses look different from normal houses. Phillips **encourages** the homeowners to be creative and make each house look **unique**.

BUILDING OF THE FUTURE?

Mexico City, Mexico

What happens when you need a lot more living space, but you can't build skyscrapers? That was the challenge facing architects in Mexico City, where tall buildings are forbidden in order to preserve the city's cultural heritage. The solution: Build an "Earthscraper." The Earthscraper is a pyramid-shaped tower built upside-down and under the ground. Still in the planning stage, this innovative building will provide housing, office space, and cultural centers, says architect Emilio Barjau—without affecting the city's historic downtown area.

A View Down

The current concrete plaza would become the glass roof of the Earthscraper.

Moving Around

Hanging platforms will transport people up and down to key floors.

Live, Work, and Play

The first ten floors will be a museum featuring artifacts discovered during the digging. Below that will be a shopping mall, restaurants, and a movie theater. The rest of the floors will be offices and apartments. Gardens and parks will be located every ten floors.

Mexico City today

Aztec Ceremonial Complex

+ 0.00

10 STOREYS MUSEUM

- 60.00

10 STOREYS RETAIL

- 100.00

10 STOREYS LIVING SPACES

- 140.00

- 180.00

35 STOREYS OFFICE SPACE

- 220.00

- 260.00

SECTION A-A

M&E

- 300.00

82

Builder Dan Phillips stands next to a house made from recycled wood. Phillips believes that there is a lot of waste in the building industry.

Developing Reading Skills

GETTING THE MAIN IDEAS

What is the main idea of the passage on pages 80–82? Complete the statement.

People are using _____ to create places to live and work.

a. modern materials and nonprofessional builders
b. available resources and adapting to local conditions
c. abandoned homes and office buildings

ORGANIZING SUPPORTING DETAILS

One way to understand and remember supporting details is to organize them in a chart.

Complete the chart using the information below. Refer to the passage on pages 80–82.

a. Caracas, Venezuela
b. an underground building
c. materials thrown away by building companies
d. Huntsville, Texas
e. a building abandoned by a construction company
f. empty offices
g. glass for a roof
h. houses made from recycled wood
i. Mexico City

	City in a Tower	Recycled Homes	Earthscraper
Location:	___	___	___
Description:	___	___	___
Materials:	*f*	___	___

UNDERSTANDING REASONS

Writers often use reasons that explain cause and effect relationships. They use words like *because, so, therefore*, and *since*. Some words come before the reason *(since, because),* and others come after or before a result *(so, therefore)*.

Complete the chart by matching each reason below with the correct idea.

a. He thinks throwing away materials is a waste.
b. There are no elevators.
c. The construction company closed.
d. They can't build up.
e. The local people are not professional builders.

Idea	Reason
1. Torre David was empty.	____
2. Taxis take people to the higher floors of Torre David.	____
3. Dan Phillips wants to build houses with unused materials.	____
4. Dan Phillips provides help with building skills.	____
5. The Earthscraper architects plan to build underground.	____

BUILDING VOCABULARY

A. **Choose the best word to complete each sentence.**

community   materials   residents   unique

1. Each of Phillips's houses is _____ because each one has a special style that is unlike any other.

2. _____ for building houses include concrete, wood, and cement.

3. People who live in Torre David like to help each other. For example, many people in the _____ helped to plant trees.

4. Some _____ of Torre David opened a store in the building. These people are able to live and work in the same place.

B. **Match each word with the correct definition.**

___ **1.** construction   **a.** to give someone hope or confidence

___ **2.** encourage   **b.** relating to work that requires special training

___ **3.** professional   **c.** the act of building something

___ **4.** technique   **d.** a method or procedure for doing something

GETTING MEANING FROM CONTEXT

A. **The writer says that people have found creative ways to *make the most of* the resources they have. What do you think this phrase means? Choose the correct answer.**

a. To create something that didn't exist before
b. To make something bigger or more important
c. To get as much value as is possible out of something

B. **In paragraph 1, the writer says the local residents *saw an opportunity*. What do you think this phrase means? Share your ideas with a partner. Then, choose the best way to complete the sentence below.**

There was an abandoned building in the neighborhood. A resident noticed it and saw an opportunity. So she ___.

a. turned it into a shop that sold things people needed
b. looked to see what was behind it
c. thought it was a terrible waste

CRITICAL THINKING

1. Synthesizing. What are three things the buildings in the reading passage have in common?

_____

_____

_____

2. Analyzing. What are some possible problems with living in one of the places described in the passage?

_____

_____

_____

EXPLORE MORE

Watch Dan Phillips's TED Talk at TED.com. What else makes his buildings unique? Share what you learn with your class.

TEDTALKS

INGENIOUS HOMES IN UNEXPECTED PLACES

IWAN BAAN Urban documentarian, TED speaker

🏠 Iwan Baan is a Dutch photographer who takes photos of buildings.

Baan has worked with some of the most famous architects in the world. But he isn't only interested in the things that architects build. In fact, he's much more interested in how ordinary people create spaces to live and work. He especially likes to focus on people in poorer countries, where infrastructure such as housing, electricity, and clean drinking water is often lacking. Baan documents how people adapt to their environments when these resources are not available. His photos show the creative ways that people make their own communities using whatever resources they have at hand.

---

document: *v.* to make a record of something

infrastructure: *n.* roads, water, electricity, and other basic things that help a country's people and economy

In this lesson, you are going to watch segments of Baan's TED Talk. Use the information about Baan above to answer the questions.

1. What is Baan's profession?

   _____

2. What is Baan most interested in?

   _____

3. What do Baan's photographs show?

   _____

Baan's **idea worth spreading** is that humans can make homes anywhere, and design spaces to make the most of their circumstances.

The floating community of Makoko, Nigeria.
Photograph by Iwan Baan.

PART 1

A HOME ON THE WATER

PREVIEWING

A. **Read the excerpt below from Baan's talk. Complete the paragraph with the words below.**

adapted   appear   become   located

Let's go now to Africa, to Nigeria, to a community called Makoko, a slum where 150,000 people live just

meters above the Lagos Lagoon. While it may _____ to be a completely chaotic place, when you see

it from above, there seems to be a whole grid of waterways and canals connecting each and every home.

From the main dock, people board long wooden canoes which carry them out to their various homes and

shops _____ in the expansive area. When out on the water, it's clear that life has been completely

_____ to this very specific way of living. Even the canoes _____ variety stores where ladies

paddle from house to house, selling anything from toothpaste to fresh fruits.

---

chaotic: *adj.* extremely disorganized; not having order   **slum:** *n.* part of a city where poor people live in bad housing

B.   Watch (▶) the first segment of Baan's TED Talk, and check your answers to
     Exercise A.

GETTING THE MAIN IDEA

**What is the most important idea in this segment of Baan's TED Talk? Complete the
statement using the best phrase below (a–c).**

People in Makoko have adapted to their environment by _____.

a. using unusual materials to create their homes
b. building an entire community on the water
c. developing new types of transportation to get from place to place

UNDERSTANDING KEY DETAILS

A.   **How have people in Makoko adapted to their environment? Complete the concept map
     with the letters of the words and expressions below.**

a. a floating band   **d.** canoes
b. a floating school   **e.** fishing
c. boat-making   **f.** floating stores

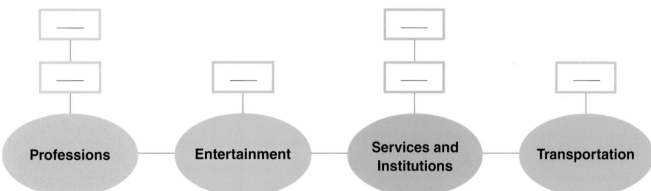

B.   **Use information from Baan's talk to add an extra detail to each category in the concept
     map above.**

CRITICAL THINKING

Inferring. Read Baan's comment about Makoko below. Why do you think the people of Makoko
decided to create a community on the water?

❝ The population growth in Nigeria, and especially in these areas like Makoko, are painful
reminders of how out of control things really are. ❞

PART 2

BRILLIANT FORMS OF INGENUITY

UNDERSTANDING MAIN IDEAS

Watch (▶) the next segment of Baan's TED Talk, and complete the sentences below.

1. Baan says that these communities could create even better solutions if _____.

   a. experts gave them some training in architecture

   b. they had some basic infrastructure to build from

   c. their governments provided most of their housing

2. Baan thinks that many large residential building projects around the world are _____.

   a. creative and convenient places to live

   b. being abandoned as soon as they are built

   c. not creative and do not provide what people need

RECOGNIZING ATTITUDE

A. **Read this excerpt from Baan's talk and underline the adjectives.**

❝ In most of these places, the government is completely absent, leaving inhabitants with no choice but to reappropriate found materials, and while these communities are highly disadvantaged, they do present examples of brilliant forms of ingenuity and prove that indeed we have the ability to adapt to all manner of circumstances. What makes places like the Torre David particularly remarkable is this sort of skeleton framework where people can have a foundation where they can tap into. Now imagine what these already ingenious communities could create themselves, and how highly particular their solutions would be, if they were given the basic infrastructures that they could tap into. **❯❯**

---

reappropriate: *v.* take and use for a new purpose   **tap into:** *v.* make use of

B. **Does Baan have a positive or negative attitude toward the communities he documents? How do you know? Discuss your ideas with a partner.**

CRITICAL THINKING

Applying. Baan quotes Zita Cobb: "there's this plague of sameness which is killing the human joy." Do you know any places with this problem? How could they be improved? Discuss with a partner.

EXPLORE MORE

Watch Baan's complete TED Talk at TED.com. What other unusual communities does he talk about? Share what you learn with your class.

Project

A house built between rocks in Brittany, France.

A. Work with a partner. You are going to find out about other unusual structures.

1. Go to TED.com and find the following TED Talks.

   Diébédo Francis Kéré, *How to build with clay . . . and community*

   Xavier Vilalta, *Architecture at home in its community*

   Liz Diller, *The Blur Building and other tech-empowered architecture*

   Magnus Larsson, *Turning dunes into architecture*

2. With your partner, choose one of the TED Talks, and then answer these questions about it.

   - Where is the structure?
   - What is its purpose?
   - What materials did the builders use?
   - Why is it unusual?
   - What lessons could others learn from this structure?

3. Use your information to create a two-minute presentation. Use maps, photos, and video to explain your information.

B. Work with two other pairs.

   - Give your presentations.
   - As you listen, take notes. At the end, review your notes.
   - Discuss: Which structure(s) is / are the most innovative? Why?

EXPLORE MORE

Find out about unusual housing in the city or country you live in. Share what you learn with your class.

ROADS TO FAME

GOALS

IN THIS UNIT, YOU WILL:

- Read about an online video that went viral.
- Learn about why certain videos become world famous.
- Explore other videos that went viral.

THINK AND DISCUSS

1. Would you like to be famous? Why or why not?

2. Do you think it's easier to become famous today than in the past? Why or why not?

Singer David Bowie performs at a concert in Chile. Bowie's song "Fame" describes the problems of being famous.

PRE-READING

A. What kinds of videos become popular on the Internet? Have you ever shared videos online? Note your ideas and share with a partner.

_____

_____

_____

_____

B. Look at the opening quote from Andy Warhol on page 95. What do you think he means? Is his statement becoming true? Share your ideas with a partner.

C. Look at the title, headings, and graph on pages 95–96. What do you think the reading is about? Choose the best answer(s) to complete the statement.

This passage is about _____.

a. how famous musicians sell their music online

b. how the quality of videos online is getting worse

c. how a young singer became famous online very quickly

Over 6 billion hours of video are watched each month on YouTube—that's almost an hour for every person on Earth.

GOING VIRAL

In 1968 the artist Andy Warhol **predicted**, "In the future, everybody will be world-famous for 15 minutes." Today, it seems his prediction is becoming true.

1. The tune is simple, and the lyrics don't **make sense**. But in 2011, 13-year-old Rebecca Black's song "Friday" became a **sensation**. Black recorded the song as a music video for a small record company. The company **posted** it on YouTube. In its first month online, very few people saw it. Then a popular blogger wrote about the video. He called "Friday" the worst video ever made.

200 MILLION VIEWS

2 **Suddenly**, the video went viral. Everyone wanted to see if "Friday" was really so bad. People often watched the video on Friday. Soon, other people posted similar music videos, inspired by "Friday." For example, a famous comedian posted a video called "Thursday." It had the same tune but different words. Its lyrics didn't make sense either, but they were very funny. By the end of 2011, "Friday" had over 200 million views. It was one of the most-watched videos on YouTube. Black was famous.

INSTANT FAME

3 In the 21st century, our **definition** of fame has changed. Online video-sharing sites like YouTube make it possible for ordinary people—instead of movie companies or magazines, for example—to decide who is famous. We all now have more ownership of our own pop culture, and no-one has to green-light our ideas—you can upload your own videos or publish your own work at any time. However, this fame may not be based on any actual **talent**. You could be famous for being a very bad singer or just doing something ridiculous. For some people, this can mean that fame happens when we don't **expect** it or even when we don't want it.

4 Realistically, though, your chances of becoming famous are still fairly small. In fact, 90 percent of videos viewed on YouTube are of people, like pop stars, who are already famous.

---

tune: *n.* the melody or music of a song

lyrics: *n.* the words of a song

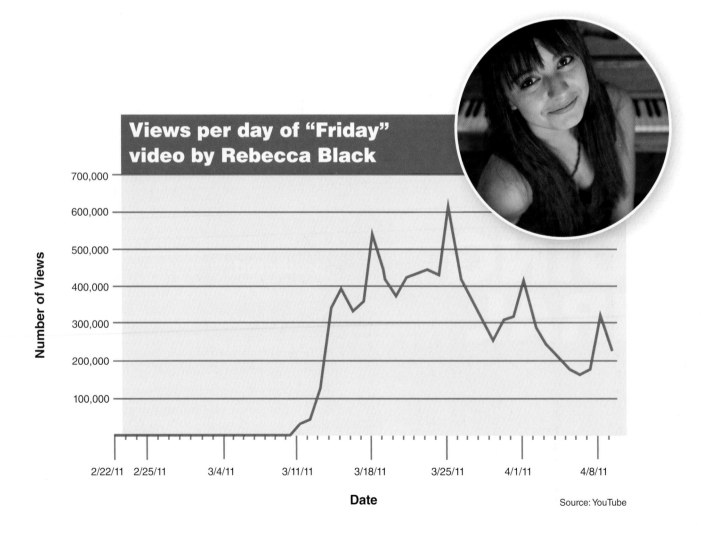

Views per day of "Friday" video by Rebecca Black

Number of Views: 700,000 / 600,000 / 500,000 / 400,000 / 300,000 / 200,000 / 100,000

Date: 2/22/11 2/25/11 3/4/11 3/11/11 3/18/11 3/25/11 4/1/11 4/8/11

Source: YouTube

Developing Reading Skills

GETTING THE MAIN IDEAS

Use information from the passage on pages 95–96 to answer each question.

1. What is the main idea of the passage? Choose the best answer.

   a. People can make their own music videos and put them on the Internet.

   b. Anyone has a chance to be famous today.

   c. Becoming famous is harder now because there is so much competition.

2. Why did Black's video suddenly become popular?

   a. People realized it was a good video to watch on Friday.

   b. People heard that the video was bad and wanted to see it.

   c. People liked Rebecca Black's other videos.

3. According to the reading passage, how has fame changed in the 21ˢᵗ century?

   _____

   _____

SCANNING FOR NUMBERS

What information did the passage on pages 95–96 include? Write *T* for True or *F* for False for each statement. If the statement is false, correct it.

_____ 1. Andy Warhol predicted everyone would be famous for 50 minutes.

_____ 2. Rebecca Black was 13 years old when she made the video "Friday."

_____ 3. By the end of 2011, Black's video had almost 200,000 views.

_____ 4. Ninety percent of videos viewed on YouTube are of people who are already stars.

UNDERSTANDING A GRAPH

A. Look again at the graph on page 96. Based on the reading, what are the dates when the following events happened?

   _____ 1. "Friday" first posted on YouTube.

   _____ 2. Blogger writes that "Friday" is the worst video ever.

   _____ 3. Over 600,000 views of "Friday" on one day.

B. How many weeks did it take for "Friday" to go from almost no views per day to over 600,000 views per day?

   _____

IDENTIFYING TRANSITION WORDS

Writers use transition words when they want to connect (*and*) or contrast (*but*) two ideas. Identifying transition words lets you connect ideas as you read.

A. **Find and underline the following sentences in the passage on pages 95–96.**

    1. A sentence that connects ideas using *and*. (Paragraph 1)
    2. Two sentences that connect ideas using *but*. (Paragraph 2)
    3. A sentence that connects ideas using *and*. (Paragraph 3)

B. **Write *and* or *but* to complete the sentences.**

    1. Many people become famous on the Internet, _____ the fame doesn't usually last.

    2. A small record company made the video _____ posted it on YouTube.

    3. The video went viral, _____ people started to post videos like it.

GETTING MEANING FROM CONTEXT

A. **The writer explains how Rebecca Black's video "went viral."**
    How would you define "went viral"?

_____

_____

B. **The writer says that today, no one has to "green-light" your ideas. What does "green-light" mean? What's another way of expressing the same idea?**

_____

_____

BUILDING VOCABULARY

A. **Complete each sentence with the correct form of the bold word or expression from the passage on pages 95–96.**

    1. When something _____, it is easy to understand.

    2. _____ is a special ability that lets you do something well.

    3. A _____ is the meaning of a word or an idea.

    4. To _____ something is to say that it will happen in the future.

B. **Read about another video that went viral. Complete the paragraph with the words below.**

expected	**posted**	**sensation**	**suddenly**

"Gangnam Style," by Korean star Psy, was released in July 2012. He _____ the song to be a hit in Korea, but the video for the song also became a worldwide _____. While popular in his own country, Psy was not well known in the rest of the world. But a week after releasing the video for the song, a famous rapper tweeted about how great the video was. _____, many other famous people _____ messages about the video. Millions of people read the messages and went to view the video on YouTube. Within days, "Gangnam Style" went viral. Today, the video has been watched over 2 billion times.

In 2012, Psy's "Gangnam Style" became the first music video to exceed one billion views on YouTube.

CRITICAL THINKING

1. Inferring. Do you think Black liked her instant fame? Why or why not?

_____

_____

2. Personalizing. Which people in your country can influence whether someone becomes famous?

_____

_____

EXPLORE MORE

Find and watch Rebecca Black's "Friday" video on YouTube.com. What do *you* think of the video? Do you agree with the blogger that it's the worst video ever?

TEDTALKS

WHY VIDEOS GO VIRAL

KEVIN ALLOCCA YouTube Trends Manager, TED speaker

Allocca's job is to watch videos. But he doesn't just watch them for pleasure. He pays attention to videos that are becoming very popular, or "going viral." In 2014, YouTube had more than 1 billion users a month. And those users uploaded dozens of hours of video every minute. Only a small percentage of these videos actually become Internet sensations.

It is hard to predict which videos will go viral, but Allocca has interesting ideas about why some videos are more popular than others.

***

user: *n.* a person who uses a product or service

In this lesson, you are going to watch Allocca's TED Talk from 2011. Use the information above to answer the questions.

1. What does Kevin Allocca do in his job?

   _____

2. How many users visited YouTube every month in 2014?

   _____

3. Is it easy to predict which videos will go viral? What ideas do you think Allocca has?

   _____

   _____

   _____

Kevin Allocca's **idea worth spreading** is that the future of entertainment is one where everyone feels ownership over pop culture and can play a role in shaping both the content and its popularity.

Singer Elvis Presley surrounded by fans, 1956.

PART 1

TASTEMAKERS

PREVIEWING

A. Scan the excerpt below from Allocca's TED Talk. What do you think Allocca means when he says that viral videos become a "cultural moment"?

_____

❝ Any one of you could be famous on the Internet by next Saturday. But there are over 48 hours of video uploaded to YouTube every minute. And of that, only a tiny percentage ever goes viral and gets tons of views and becomes a cultural moment. So how does it happen? Three things: tastemakers, communities of participation, and unexpectedness. ❞

_____

tastemaker: _n._ a person who introduces other people to things that are fashionable

B. Read the excerpt again. Circle the three things that make a video go viral. What do these three things mean, and how do you think they help videos go viral? Discuss with a partner.

GETTING THE MAIN IDEAS

A. Watch (▶) the first part of Kevin Allocca's TED Talk. What is the purpose of this segment of Allocca's TED Talk? Choose the two best statements.

    a. To introduce his ideas about why videos go viral

    b. To show how some videos make us feel sad

    c. To explain how a tastemaker can influence others

B. How did Bear Vasquez video go viral? Check (✓) the three steps that Allocca mentions in his talk.

_____ **1.** Vasquez posted his video on YouTube.

_____ **2.** Vasquez told his friends about the video.

_____ **3.** Jimmy Kimmel, a tastemaker, tweeted about the video.

_____ **4.** Kimmel put the video on his website.

_____ **5.** Millions of people watched Vasquez video.

PART 2

PARTICIPATION

PREVIEWING

A. Read the excerpt from the next segment of Allocca's TED Talk. What do you think the missing words are?

❝ But what's important here is the _____ that [the video clip] inspired amongst

this techie, geeky Internet culture. An entire remix community sprouted up that brought it

from being just a stupid _____ to something that we can all actually be a part of.

Because we don't just enjoy now, we _____. ❯❯

---

techie: *adj.* very interested in technology

geeky: *adj.* of a person who is very interested in a particular hobby, especially computers

sprouted up: *v.* grew up

B. Now watch (▶) the next segment of Allocca's TED Talk, and check your answers. According to Allocca, which video inspired people to participate in a remix community?

_____ **a.** "Friday"

_____ **b.** "Nyan Cat"

RECOGNIZING THE SPEAKER'S MESSAGE

Complete the sentence using Allocca's ideas from this segment of his talk.

People don't just sit and watch a video, they also _____ .

PART 3

UNEXPECTEDNESS

UNDERSTANDING KEY DETAILS

Read the sentences. Then watch (▶) this segment of Kevin Allocca's TED Talk.
Check (✔) the ones that reflect what he says.

☐ 1. Videos that are surprising are likely to go viral.

☐ 3. It was easy to predict Casey Niestadt's video would go viral.

☐ 2. Unique and unexpected videos stand out more.

☐ 4. The audience now decides the popularity of a video.

USING VISUALS TO SUMMARIZE

A. Complete the graphic organizer with the information you learned from Allocca's TED Talk.

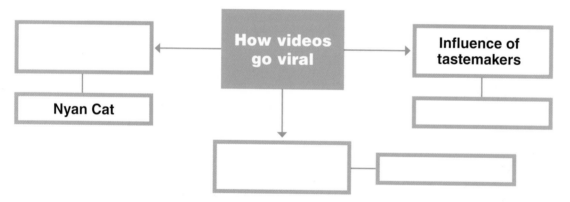

B. What other factors can help make a video go viral? Discuss your ideas with a partner.

CRITICAL THINKING

Applying. Allocca says, "[W]e don't just enjoy now, we participate." What are some other ways people participate online? Discuss with a partner.

EXPLORE MORE

View Kevin Allocca's full TED Talk at TED.com. Which of the YouTube videos would you share with your friends? Why?

Project

An image taken from Eric Whitacre's YouTube video, Virtual Choir 2.0, which went viral in 2011. In the video, Whitacre conducts over 2,000 voices from 58 countries.

A. You are going to research a video that went viral.

1. Work with a partner. Choose a video that you know that went viral. Or use one of the videos below.

   - David Blaine, *How I held my breath for 17 minutes* (TED.com)
   - *7 Billion* (video.nationalgeographic.com)
   - Eric Whitacre, *A virtual choir* (TED.com)

2. Watch the video and ask yourselves these questions:

   - What is unexpected about the video?
   - Why do you think the video went viral?

3. Make a list of ways that people could "participate" with this video. Think about Kevin Allocca's ideas from his TED Talk.

B. Present your video to your class. Explain why you think it went viral.

C. As a class, discuss which video you would share with your friends.

EXPLORE MORE

Find out what videos are trending now at youtube-trends.blogspot.com. Share what you learned with your class.

FACE OFF

IN THIS UNIT, YOU WILL:

- Read why humans and lions are in conflict.
- Learn how a 13-year-old boy stopped lion attacks on his farm.
- Explore ways that humans and big cats can live safely together.

THINK AND DISCUSS

1. Why do humans sometimes kill big cats, such as lions and tigers?

2. In what ways do big cats cause problems for humans?

Top predator: Across Africa, there are about 550–700 attacks by lions on humans each year.

PRE-READING

A. Look at the information on page 110. Discuss these questions with a partner.

1. In which parts of Africa are lions mainly found today?

   _____

   _____

2. By how much did Africa's lion population decrease between the 1800s and 1990s?

   _____

3. What might be some reasons for the fall in lion population?

   _____

   _____

   _____

B. Skim the passage quickly and answer the questions with a partner. Check your ideas as you read the passage.

1. What kind of reading passage is this? How do you know?

   ☐ Scientific article
   ☐ News report
   ☐ Personal narrative

2. What country does the passage mention? What do you think you will read about?

   _____

   _____

   _____

   _____

NEWSWATCH June 21, 2012

LIONS KILLED NEAR NAIROBI

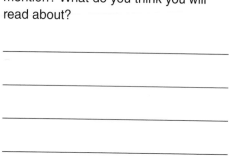

1 Yesterday morning, six lions were killed in Kitengela, just 15 kilometers south of Nairobi National Park. The killings have sent shock waves across Kenya and around the world.

2   Nairobi National Park is one of the most visited protected areas in Africa. The park is just a ten-minute ride from downtown Nairobi, and is therefore a popular tourist destination. However, the park's location close to residential areas and farmlands has led to **conflicts** between farmers and lions.

3   Part of the problem is that the park is fenced only to the east, north, and west—the sides closest to the city. Consequently, zebras and other **wild** animals are able to **migrate** across the park's unfenced southern border. Lions and other predators follow them. Some cross into residential areas such as Kitengela, and kill farmers' livestock. As a result, the farmers become angry and kill the big cats. This seems to be the cause of the latest killings.

4   The Kenyan **government** says it will find and arrest the killers of the Kitengela Six. Local community leaders, however, argue that the government does not really **take seriously** the farmers'

livestock losses. Because of this conflict, says conservationist Paula Kahumbu, Kenya must find "a lasting solution that will enable people to **benefit** from living lions."

5   Kahumbu and other conservationists are **afraid** for the lions' future. For much of the past decade, Kenya has been losing 100 lions a year. This is largely due to habitat loss, but also because of lion killings. Unless there is a way to **solve** the human–lion conflict, Kenya's lions could disappear in 20 years.

---

residential areas: *n.* areas of land where many people live

livestock: *n.* animals such as cows and sheep that are kept on a farm

arrest: *v.* (to) catch and hold someone by law

conservationist: *n.* a person who acts to protect the environment or wildlife

habitat: *n.* the natural home or environment of an animal or a plant

LIONS IN DECLINE

- There are fewer than 40,000 lions in Africa.
- Kenya's lion population has fallen from 20,000 to fewer than 2,000 in the past 50 years.
- About a quarter of Africa's lions are in four well-protected reserves; the rest are in areas where they may come into contact with humans.

Lion Population Over Time

1800s	1,200,000
1940s	450,000
1980s	100,000
1990s	50,000
2000s	20,000
2020	?

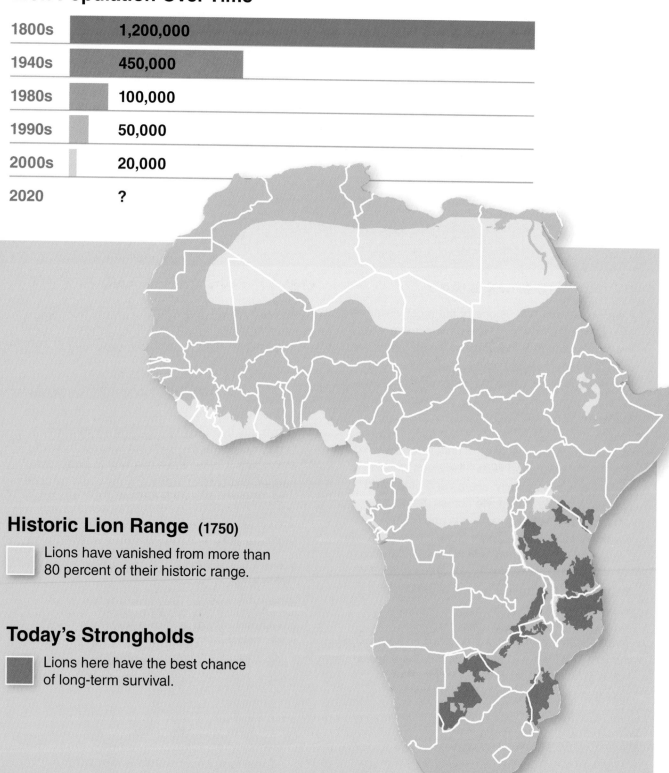

Historic Lion Range (1750)

Lions have vanished from more than 80 percent of their historic range.

Today's Strongholds

Lions here have the best chance of long-term survival.

In Nairobi, wildlife roams freely against an urban backdrop of skyscrapers.

Developing Reading Skills

GETTING THE MAIN IDEAS

Use information from the passage on pages 108–109 to answer each question.

1. What is the main problem described in the passage?

    a. A recent attack by a lion on livestock farmers

    b. The killing of lions by angry livestock farmers

    c. The falling population of livestock in Kenya

2. Who are the Kitengela Six?

    a. A team of conservationists

    b. Some lions killed by farmers

    c. A group of local community leaders

3. Who is Paula Kahumbu?
    How does she feel about the problem?

    _____

    _____

    _____

IDENTIFYING CAUSE AND EFFECT

A writer may include one or more reasons to explain why an action happens. The reason (or cause) may come before or after the action (or effect). Words that introduce reasons include *because (of)* and *due to*; words that introduce effects include *leads/led to, as a result, consequently,* and *therefore.*

A.   Scan the passage on pages 108–109, and circle any words that introduce reasons or effects.

B.   Match each cause (1–4) from the passage with an effect (a–d).

CAUSE

1. Sometimes lions kill livestock. _____
2. The park is fenced only on three sides. _____
3. The park is easy to travel to from Nairobi. _____
4. Lions are losing their habitat. _____

EFFECT

    a. The park is very popular with tourists.

    b. Animals cross the park's southern border.

    c. Lion populations are falling fast.

    d. Farmers get angry and kill lions.

VISUALIZING DETAILS

Use information from the passage to label the map (a–e). Then add an arrow to show the direction of the lions' migration.

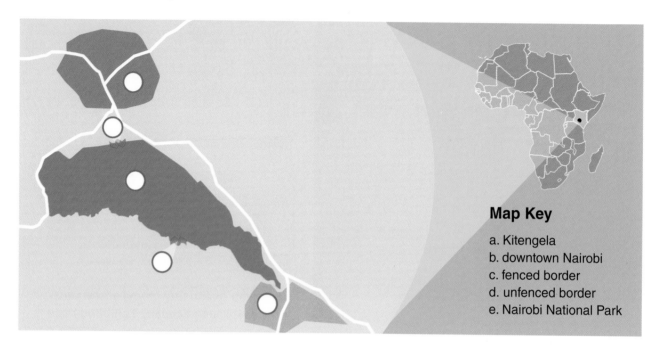

Map Key

a. Kitengela
b. downtown Nairobi
c. fenced border
d. unfenced border
e. Nairobi National Park

BUILDING VOCABULARY

A. Choose the best word to complete each sentence.

> benefit　　government　　migrate　　wild

1. Some animals _____ to warmer areas during winter months.

2. A _____ animal lives in a natural environment and is not looked after by people.

3. If you _____ from something, it helps you or improves your life.

4. The _____ is the group of people who lead a country.

B. Choose the best option(s) to answer each question.

1. Which of these might you try to **solve**?

　a. an area　　　　b. a border　　　　c. a problem

2. Which of these are people most likely to **take seriously**?

　a. their health　　b. a TV comedy　　c. a cup of coffee

3. Which of these is a person most likely to be **afraid** of?

　a. a butterfly　　b. a lion　　　　c. a zebra

4. Which two of these are examples of **conflicts**?

　a. an argument　　b. an earthquake　　c. a war

GETTING MEANING FROM CONTEXT

The writer says the killing of the Kitengela Six "sent shock waves" across Kenya. What do you think the writer means? How else could you express this idea?

_____

_____

UNDERSTANDING INFOGRAPHICS

Use information from the infographic on page 110 to complete each sentence.

1. Today, there are no lion strongholds in _____.

   a. East Africa   b. West Africa   c. Southern Africa

2. The population of African lions fell below half a million in _____.

   a. the late 1800s   b. the early 1940s   c. the mid-1980s

3. There are now about _____ lions in Kenya.

   a. 2,000   b. 20,000   c. 50,000

4. The percentage of Africa's lions living in reserves is about _____.

   a. 25%   b. 50%   c. 75%

CRITICAL THINKING

1. Reasoning. What do you think the Kenyan government should do with the killers of the Kitengela Six? Why do you think so?

_____

_____

_____

2. Reflecting. Paula Kahumbu says there is a need for a "lasting solution." What might be a possible solution to the problem?

_____

_____

_____

EXPLORE MORE

Read more about Paula Kahumbu at nationalgeographic.com. Share what you learn with the class.

TEDTALKS

MY INVENTION THAT MADE PEACE WITH LIONS

RICHARD TURERE Inventor, TED speaker

🎧 Richard Turere is a young Kenyan man from Kitengela, a farming community on the edge of Nairobi National Park.

Since the age of nine, Turere has helped to look after his family's cattle, which the family keeps in a cowshed. In his free time, Turere enjoys playing with electronics. As a child, he began making his own inventions. He made fans from car parts and other items. He also built other electronic devices for his neighbors.

At the age of 13, Turere invented something that changed his life. It also changed the lives of many people in his community. One night, a lion from the neighboring park came into his family's farm and killed one of their cows. Turere was angry. However, killing the lion, he thought, was not the best way to solve the problem. Instead, he decided to invent a solution.

---

cowshed: *n.* a farm building in which cattle are kept

electronic devices: *n.* equipment such as calculators, computers, and radios

In this lesson, you are going to watch segments from Turere's TED Talk. Use the information above to answer the questions on page 115.

Richard Turere's **idea worth spreading** is that no matter how old you are, anyone can be an inventor and make a meaningful impact on a community.

1. As a child, how did Turere help his family?

   _____

2. What is Turere interested in?

   _____

3. What made Turere angry when he was 13?

   _____

Richard Turere attaches his flashing "lion lights" to a cattle fence near Nairobi National Park.

PART 1

THE PROBLEM WITH LIONS

PREVIEWING

A. **Scan the following excerpt from Turere's TED Talk. What were Turere's first two ideas? Underline them.**

B. **What words do you think are missing? Write a word or phrase for each gap and share with a partner.**

❝ So I had to find a way of solving this problem. And the first idea I got was to use fire, because I thought lions were _____ of fire. But I came to realize that that didn't really help, because it was even helping the lions
₁

to see through the cowshed. So I didn't give up. I continued.

And a second idea I got was to use a scarecrow. I was trying to trick the lions [into thinking] that I was

standing near the cowshed. But lions are very _____. They will come the first day and they see the
₂

scarecrow, and they go back. But the second day, they'll come and they say, this thing is not moving here, it's

always here! So he jumps in and _____ the animals.
₃

So one night, I was walking around the cowshed with a torch, and that day, the lions didn't come.

And I discovered that lions are afraid of a _____ light. So I had an idea . . . ❯❯
₄

GETTING THE MAIN IDEAS

A. Watch (▶) the first segment of Turere's TED Talk, and check your answers on page 116.

B. Why didn't Turere's first two ideas work? Note the problem for each one.

1. The lions could _____.

2. The lions noticed that _____.

CRITICAL THINKING

Predicting. What do you think was Turere's third idea? Look at the diagram of his invention on page 118. Guess: What does it do? How does it work? Note your ideas and share with a partner.

PART 2

AN INSPIRED SOLUTION

UNDERSTANDING KEY DETAILS

Read these sentences about Turere and his invention. Circle the answers as you watch (▶) the next part of his TED Talk.

1. Turere's invention works because lions are afraid of _____.

    a. the flashing light

    b. the loud noise

    c. the bright colors

2. Turere learned about electronics _____.

    a. from his parents

    b. by listening to talks on a radio

    c. by taking apart an old radio

3. Turere used a battery from a _____.

    a. car

    b. motorcycle

    c. radio

4. Other people use his invention to scare away hyenas, leopards, and _____.

    a. cheetahs

    b. elephants

    c. rhinos

RECOGNIZING TONE AND MESSAGE

1. Read the statements. Which one best matches Turere's overall message?

    a. We must do everything we can to protect lions in Africa.

    b. It's possible for humans and lions to live together without conflict.

    c. The needs of livestock farmers are more important than the needs of lions.

2. Which statement best matches Turere's attitude toward lions?

    a. I still feel very angry that a lion killed one of my family's cows.

    b. I used to hate lions, but now I've found a way to live with them.

    c. I used to think lions were okay, but now I realize how dangerous they are.

TEDTALKS

SUMMARIZING A PROCESS

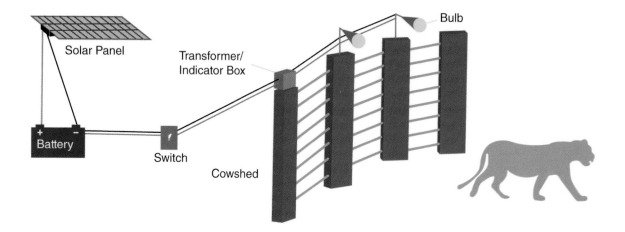

A. **Turere's invention has different parts. What do the following items (1–3) do? Match each one with a description (a–c).**

1. A battery _____

2. An indicator box _____

3. A solar panel _____

a. makes lights flash on and off.

b. provides power to make something work.

c. stores energy from the sun.

B. **Read the sentences and study the diagram. Use the steps (a–d) to complete the summary.**

1. The solar panel gets energy from the sun.

2. _____

3. _____

4. Turere turns on the switch.

5. _____

6. _____

7. The lions become afraid and run away.

a. The indicator (transformer) makes the light bulbs flash.

b. Energy from the solar panel charges the battery.

c. The flashing lights make the lions think that someone is moving.

d. The battery supplies power to the indicator box (transformer).

CRITICAL THINKING

1. Interpreting. The title of the unit is "Face Off." What does this expression mean? Can you identify at least two kinds of "face offs" in this unit? Discuss with a partner.

2. Reflecting. Imagine you could interview Richard Turere. Write 2-3 questions you would ask him.

EXPLORE MORE

Watch more of Richard Turere's TED Talk on TED.com. Share what you learn with your class. For example, how was Turere changed by his experience?

Project

In Kenya, livestock enclosures such as this one, known as a *boma*, provide a simple, cost-effective way to keep livestock safe from predators at night.

A. **Work with a partner. You are going to research another human–animal conflict.**

1. Choose an example of human–animal conflict and find answers to the following.

   What is the problem?
   Where is the problem happening?
   Why is it happening?
   What are people doing to solve the problem?
   Is it working? Why, or why not?

   For example:
   In Kenya, conflict sometimes occurs when an elephant crosses a farmer's land. Now, farmers can track the elephant migrations with a special collar. It's something an elephant wears on its neck. It uses GPS. First, the farmers put it on the animal's neck. Then . . .

2. Use your answers to create a two-minute presentation. You can use maps, photos, and video to explain your information.

B. **Work with two other pairs.**

- Give your presentations.
- As you listen, take notes.
- At the end, review your notes.
- Are the problems being solved?
- If not, what else can people do?

EXPLORE MORE

Go to TED.com to watch John Kasaona's TED Talk "How poachers became caretakers." Share what you find out with your class.

GOALS

IN THIS UNIT, YOU WILL:

- Read about a community-based art project.
- Learn more about an artist who inspires communities.
- Explore how to improve your community.

THINK AND DISCUSS

1. What is a community? What makes a community work well?

2. How can art in public spaces make communities better?

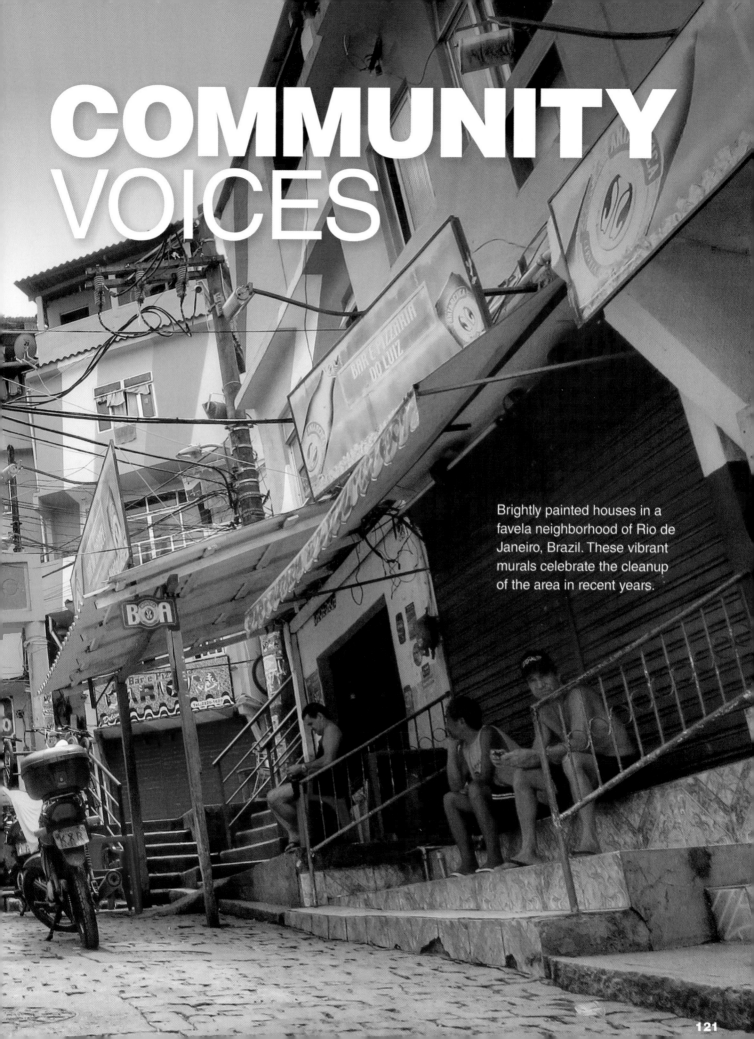

COMMUNITY
VOICES

Brightly painted houses in a favela neighborhood of Rio de Janeiro, Brazil. These vibrant murals celebrate the cleanup of the area in recent years.

Lesson A

PRE-READING

A. Skim the passage on pages 123–124. What do you think the passage is mainly about?

This passage is mainly about ___.

_____ **a.** improving a city center

_____ **b.** making an outdoor art museum

_____ **c.** an art project in a neighborhood

B. Quickly read the first and second paragraphs. What kind of art do you think Candy Chang makes?

a. Sculptures that people can climb on

b. Art that people can interact with

c. Paintings that people can buy

C. Look at the photo. Why do you think people are writing on the stickers?

_____

_____

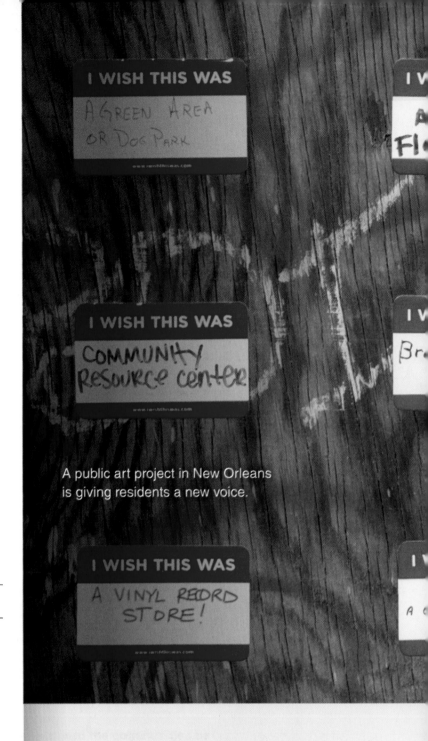

A public art project in New Orleans is giving residents a new voice.

122

ART IN THE COMMUNITY

1 On a street in New Orleans is an old building. It used to be a grocery store. But now it is vacant. On the boards covering the windows are **stickers**. Each sticker says "I wish this was . . ." Someone has written "full of food" on one of the stickers.

2   When we think of **public** art, we often think of sculptures or other large works of art in city centers. Candy Chang's public art, however, is somewhere else. Chang makes her art in a city's older or poorer **neighborhoods**. She uses the outside walls of vacant buildings as her canvas. She paints, writes **messages**, or puts stickers on them. Chang wants to **reach out** to people with her art. She sees it as the start of a conversation—a conversation with local residents.

3   In 2010, Chang started the "I Wish This Was" project in New Orleans. Chang asked residents to look at the abandoned buildings in their community. She wanted them to think about what else could be there. She printed hundreds of small stickers and stuck them on these buildings. The stickers said, "I wish this was" in large letters and included a space for people to write. Anyone could write anything.

Chang was amazed at the **reaction**. Hundreds of residents wrote on the stickers. Someone wrote, "I wish this was a grocery store." Another person wrote, "I wish this was Heaven."

4   There are many **abandoned** buildings in neighborhoods around the world. It's hard for residents to create a close neighborhood if the streets are full of empty buildings. By making art that gives residents a voice, Chang hopes to build stronger communities. Chang's art projects get residents thinking and talking about problems in their community. This **initiative** may help city planners to create better cities—ones that truly meet the needs of residents.

---

canvas: *n.* a piece of strong cloth used for a painting

sculpture: *n.* a piece of art that is made from wood, stone, metal, etc.

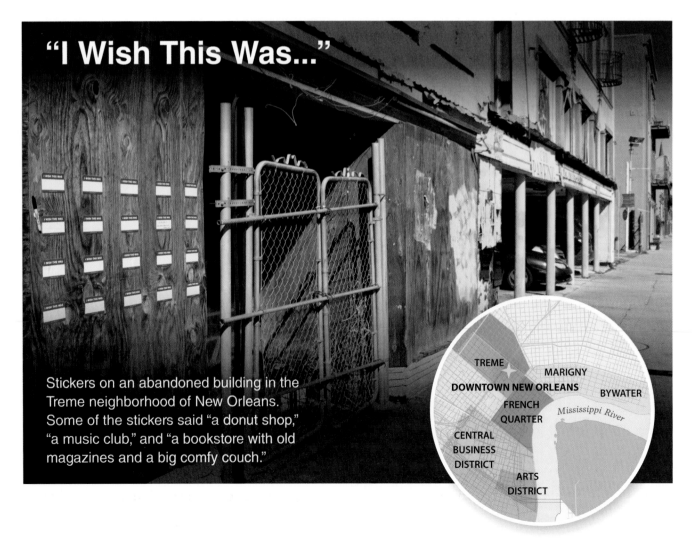

"I Wish This Was..."

Stickers on an abandoned building in the Treme neighborhood of New Orleans. Some of the stickers said "a donut shop," "a music club," and "a bookstore with old magazines and a big comfy couch."

A mural of local musician Ernie K-Doe in the Bywater district of New Orleans.

Developing Reading Skills

GETTING THE MAIN IDEAS

Use information from the passage on pages 123–124 to answer each question.

1. What does Chang hope her art projects do?

    a. Encourage people to make their own art in the community

    b. Get people thinking about how to make their community better

    c. Make people look after old buildings in their community

2. What are some ways that Chang's art project has changed the community? Check (✔) the two results mentioned in the reading.

    _____ **a.** People are converting empty buildings into new businesses.

    _____ **b.** People are talking about problems in their neighborhood.

    _____ **c.** People are imagining things they can change in their neighborhood.

UNDERSTANDING A PARAGRAPH'S PURPOSE

Writers organize their thoughts into paragraphs so that readers can understand them better. When we read, it's useful to understand what a writer's purpose is for each paragraph.

1. What is the purpose of paragraph 1?

    a. To set the scene for the reading

    b. To give an opinion about an event in New Orleans

2. What is the purpose of paragraph 2?

    a. To persuade us that Chang's art is good

    b. To explain Chang's reasons for creating art

3. What is the purpose of paragraph 3?

    a. To describe some of the challenges Chang faces

    b. To explain how one of Chang's art projects works

4. What is the purpose of paragraph 4?

    a. To describe the people in Chang's community

    b. To explain how Chang's art has a useful purpose

UNDERSTANDING REFERENCES

Find the following sentences in the reading. What does the underlined word refer to?

1. <u>It</u> used to be a grocery store. (Paragraph 1)

   _____

2. She paints, writes messages, or puts stickers on <u>them</u>. (Paragraph 2)

   _____

3. She wanted <u>them</u> to think about what could be there instead. (Paragraph 3)

   _____

4. . . . —<u>ones</u> that truly meet the needs of residents. (Paragraph 4)

   _____

BUILDING VOCABULARY

A. **Find the bold words in the passage on pages 123–124. Then complete the paragraph with the correct words.**

In Minnesota, artists have a new place to show their work. The Artists in Storefronts

project turns _____ or vacant storefronts into mini-galleries. Over 160 local artists

have shown their paintings, sculptures, and other artwork in empty store windows. Artists

also do interactive art projects in _____ spaces, similar to those created by Candy

Chang. The organizers hope this _____ will make _____ more attractive

and will also improve the local economy.

B. **Look again at the bold words and expressions in the passage on pages 123–124. Then match each word or expression to its definition.**

_____ **1.** reach out

_____ **2.** sticker

_____ **3.** messages

_____ **4.** reaction

a. pieces of written or spoken information

b. something you say, feel, or do as a result of something that happens

c. to try to connect with other people

d. a label with a type of glue on the back

GETTING MEANING FROM CONTEXT

1. Candy Chang hopes her art will "give residents a voice." What does "to give someone a voice" mean? How else could you say this?

    _____

2. What other ways are there to give residents in a community a voice?

    _____

CRITICAL THINKING

1. Interpreting. Why was Chang "amazed at the reaction" to her project? What reaction was she expecting?

    _____

2. Predicting. How might the neighborhood change as a result of Chang's project?

    _____

3. Applying. If you had a "I wish this was . . ." sticker, where in your city would you put it? What do you think people would write on it?

    _____

EXPLORE MORE

Go to Candy Chang's speaker profile on TED.com, and read about some of her other projects. Choose one and tell your class about it. Why was it especially interesting to you?

TEDTALKS

BEFORE I DIE, I WANT TO ...

CANDY CHANG Artist and Urban Planner, TED speaker

🔊 Candy Chang explores new ideas for the design of our cities. She creates art that prompts people to think about their secrets, wishes, and hopes—and then share them.

One of her projects, "I Wish This Was ..." encouraged residents in New Orleans to think about what they wanted to happen to abandoned and vacant buildings.

More recently, Chang created a project called "Before I Die." Chang installs a wall in a public space and encourages people to write their personal hopes and dreams on it. Chang made the first "Before I Die" wall in 2011. Since then, 500 walls have been created in over 30 languages and over 65 countries, including Kazakhstan, Japan, and Iraq. In 2013, the book *Before I Die* was published, showing these walls and the stories behind them.

In this lesson, you are going to watch segments of Chang's TED Talk. Use the information above to answer the questions.

1. Why does Candy Chang make her art?

   _____

2. What is the "Before I Die" project? How is it different from the "I Wish This Was ..." project?

   _____

   _____

3. How can you tell that the project has been successful?

   _____

   _____

Candy Chang's **idea worth spreading** is that there are many simple, surprising, and powerful ways we can share our hopes and ideas with other people in our community.

A boy adds his hopes for the future to a "Before I Die" wall in Mexico City.

INSPIRATION

PREVIEWING

A. **Scan the following excerpt from Candy Chang's TED Talk. What did Chang think she could do with the house?**

_____

❝ I live near this house, and I thought about how I could make it a nicer space for my neighborhood, and I also thought about something that changed my life forever. In 2009, I lost someone I loved very much. Her name was Joan, and she was [like] a mother to me, and her death was sudden and unexpected. **❯❯**

B. **Read the segment again. What changed Chang's life?**

_____

C. **How do you think Chang's friend's death might have "changed her life forever"? Share your ideas with a partner.**

GETTING THE MAIN IDEAS

Watch (▶) the first segment of Chang's TED Talk. What ideas does Chang express? Mark the statements *T* for True or *F* for False.

_____ **1.** Chang wanted to paint pictures of her friend who died.

_____ **2.** It's easy to forget what really matters in our lives.

_____ **3.** An abandoned house can be a place for people to share their hopes.

UNDERSTANDING KEY DETAILS

Complete these sentences about Chang's "Before I Die" project. Check your answers as you watch (▶) the first part of her talk again.

1. Chang sometimes forgets _____.

   a. the people that live in her community

   b. the important things in her life

   c. the bad things that happen to people

2. Chang created her project _____.

   a. with her friends

   b. by herself

   c. with her family

3. People filled the wall with their ideas in _____.

   a. a week

   b. a month

   c. a day

CRITICAL THINKING

1. Interpreting. Chang mentions that it is "easy to get caught up in the day-to-day." What do you think she means? How else could you say this?

   _____

   _____

2. Prediction. At the end of the segment, Chang says she'd "like to share a few things that people wrote on this wall." What kind of things do you think people wrote on the wall?

   _____

   _____

PART 2

I WANT TO PLANT A TREE

PREDICTING

In the next segment, Chang describes what she learned from the project. Read this excerpt and predict the missing words. Check your ideas as you watch (▶) the talk.

❝ [These] hopes and dreams made me _____ out loud, tear up, and they consoled me during my own tough times. It's about knowing you're not alone. It's about understanding our _____ in new and enlightening ways. It's about making _____ for reflection and contemplation, and remembering what really matters most to us as we _____ and change. ❞

RECOGNIZING THE SPEAKER'S POINT OF VIEW

Read the excerpt from Chang's TED Talk. How does she feel about public spaces? Choose the two best endings for the statement below.

❝ Together, we've shown how powerful our public spaces can be if we're given the opportunity to have a voice and share more with one another. Our shared spaces can better reflect what matters to us as individuals and as a community, and with more ways to share our hopes, fears and stories, the people around us can not only help us make better places, they can help us lead better lives. ❞

Our public spaces should _____.

a. make our lives better

b. be good for businesses

c. show what we think is important

d. be protected by the government

CRITICAL THINKING

1. Synthesizing. Is there an area near where you live that could benefit from art projects like Chang's? Give reasons for your ideas.

   _____

   _____

2. Applying. Complete the sentence about you: "Before I die, _____

   _____ ."

EXPLORE MORE

Watch Chang's complete TED Talk at TED.com. What else did you learn from her talk? Share your ideas with your class.

Project

Volunteers clean up part of the mural-covered Berlin Wall in Berlin, Germany.

Work in small groups. You are going to conduct a survey about how to improve your community.

1. Create a list of questions you want to ask your classmates. Brainstorm ideas about things that people often don't like about their communities. For example: *abandoned buildings, graffiti, crime, noise*.

2. Choose one of the ideas, and write questions to ask your classmates about what they don't like about their community. For example:

   - *How bad a problem is graffiti in your community?*
   - *What's a good way to solve this problem?*

3. Ask your classmates the questions. Ask follow-up questions to find out more details.

4. Present your results to the class.

   - Prepare a poster or chart that summarizes the answers to your questions.
   - Tell the class about interesting ideas to solve problems in the community.
   - Following Chang's example, how could you gather additional ideas from other members of your community?

EXPLORE MORE

Learn about another artist using art to change communities. Watch JR's TED Talk "One year of turning the world inside out" at TED.com. Share what you learned with your classmates.

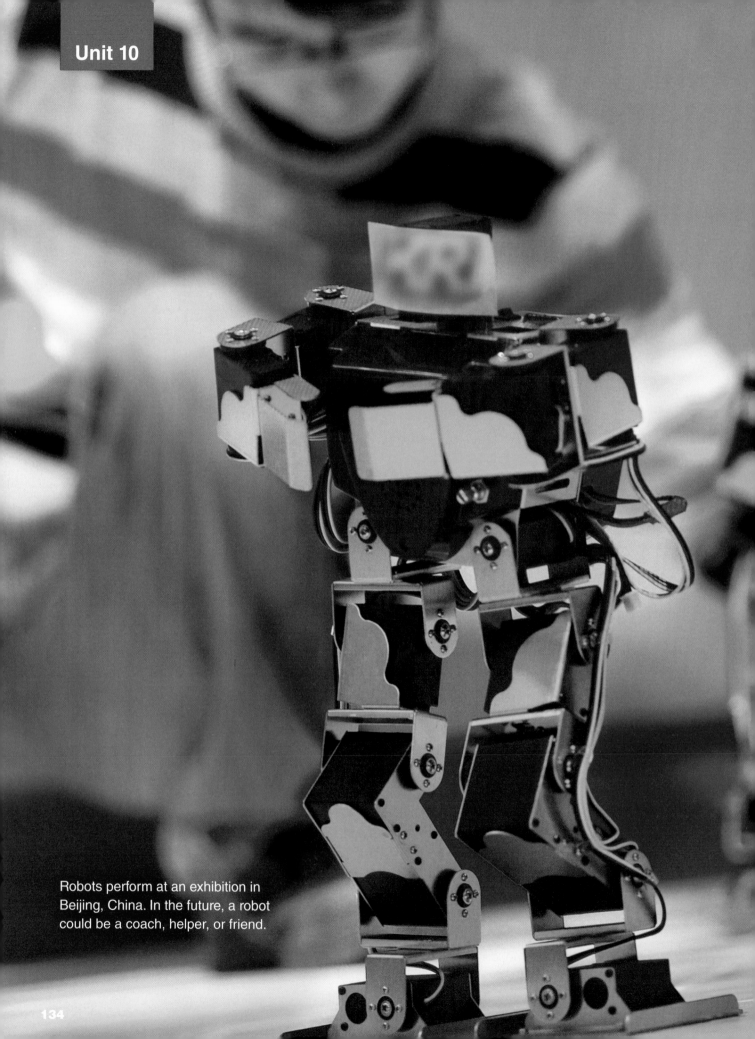

Robots perform at an exhibition in Beijing, China. In the future, a robot could be a coach, helper, or friend.

ROBOTS
AND US

IN THIS UNIT, YOU WILL:

- Read about a new kind of robot.
- Learn about robots that help people connect with one another.
- Explore different uses for robots.

THINK AND DISCUSS

1. What are some machines that make life easier? How do they improve our quality of life?

2. Think about robots that have appeared in movies, games, or books. What are they like? What do they do?

PRE-READING

A. **Look at the photos on pages 136–138, and answer the questions below.**

1. Describe what the robots look like.

_____

_____

2. What do you think Nexi and Autom can do?

_____

_____

B. **Read the first sentence of each paragraph on page 138. Choose the best answer to the question.**

What is the purpose of this passage?

a. To give an opinion about robots

b. To explain the results of a robot study

c. To describe examples of social robots

C. **In what ways do you think a robot could be a coach, helper, or friend?**

_____

_____

_____

_____

ROBOTS LIKE US

1 Meet Nexi. Nexi is one of a new **generation** of robots. It moves on wheels and can pick up objects. But robots like Nexi are more than just entertaining toys.

Nexi, a "social robot" created by scientists at the Massachusetts Institute of Technology, can express human emotions.

INTERACTING WITH ROBOTS

2 Roboticists at the Massachusetts Institute of Technology (MIT) call Nexi a "social robot." A social robot is a robot that can communicate like a human. It can **express** human **emotions**. Nexi can look sad, mad, and even bored. Social robots can also "read" our facial expressions. For example, it can see that we are sad and can say something to make us happy. Roboticists, like MIT's Cynthia Breazeal, believe that it won't be long before we have social robots in our homes, helping us live better lives.

3 Autom is another social robot **developed** at MIT. Autom is a robot health coach. It has a screen where you enter information about what food you ate that day or how much you exercised. Autom has a face with eyes that move. It speaks with a synthesized voice. Autom gives you **advice** about your diet and exercise, and **motivates** you to do better.

4 In a test, Autom helped people lose weight better than other ways of recording diet information. Breazeal thinks this is because Autom used facial expressions and words of encouragement. In other words, Autom **interacted** like a real person. In fact, many people who used Autom gave the robot a new name and talked to it. When robots use human expressions and body language, Breazeal says, people **respond** to them "a lot like they respond to people."

5 In the future, humans may interact with social robots just like they do with other people. The robot of the future will be not just a machine; it may also be your coach, helper, or friend.

---

roboticists: *n.* people who study and design robots

coach: *n.* a person who helps people achieve goals

Testing
Autom

Breazeal and her colleagues at MIT tested Autom with different groups of people. In the test, some people used Autom to record diet and exercise information. Other people recorded their food and exercise on a regular computer or with pencil and paper. The test showed that people who used Autom were healthier, exercised more, and lost more weight than the other people in the study.

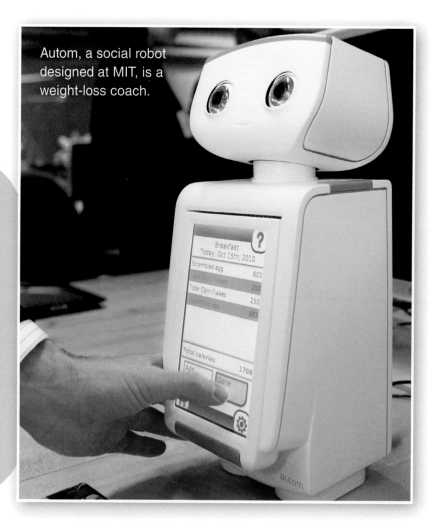

Autom, a social robot designed at MIT, is a weight-loss coach.

A still from the movie *Star Wars*. The robot R2D2 is a helper and a friend to the characters in the movie.

Developing Reading Skills

GETTING THE MAIN IDEAS

What is the main idea of the passage? Check (✓) the best sentence.

- ☐ **a.** New kinds of robots might someday help people live better lives.
- ☐ **b.** One type of social robot works like a health coach.
- ☐ **c.** Nexi moves on wheels and can pick things up.
- ☐ **d.** MIT created the "social robot."

IDENTIFYING MAIN AND SUPPORTING IDEAS IN PARAGRAPHS

Identify the main ideas (M) and the supporting ideas (S) for paragraphs 2, 3, and 4 of the passage.

Paragraph 2

1. _____ A social robot can communicate like a human.

2. _____ One type of social robot is Nexi.

3. _____ Nexi can read people's facial expressions and respond to them.

Paragraph 3

4. _____ Autom is a health coach.

5. _____ Autom takes information about a person's diet and exercise, and gives advice and encouragement.

6. _____ Autom is another type of social robot.

Paragraph 4

7. _____ People treated Autom like a person.

8. _____ Autom interacts like a person.

9. _____ A study showed that people who used Autom to improve health had good results.

MAKING COMPARISONS

How are Nexi and Autom similar? How are they different? Work with a partner to complete the Venn diagram using the information below.

a. has a face
b. gives advice
c. reads facial expressions
d. can look sad, mad, or bored
e. speaks
f. motivates people to lose weight

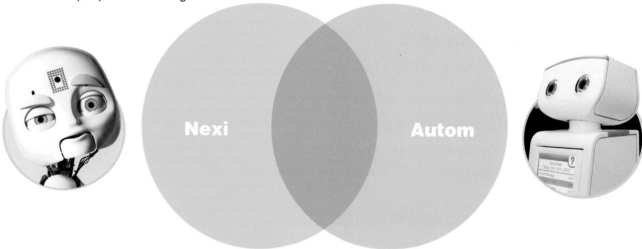

Nexi   Autom

BUILDING VOCABULARY

A. **Choose the correct word to complete each sentence.**

1. Nexi can **respond / express** to you just like a person and can say things to make you feel better.

2. Some people cannot **develop / express** their feelings when they talk, but they can explain them well when they write.

3. If you want to **motivate / develop** people who are trying to lose weight, it's important to encourage them.

4. University researchers hope to **express / develop** new technologies like robots.

5. If a robot doesn't **interact / express** in the same way as a human, people may not feel very comfortable with it in their homes.

B. **Complete the sentences with the correct words.**

advice   emotion   generation

1. Studies show that people feel more comfortable with robots that can show a/an _____ such as happiness or sadness.

2. Social robots are called "a new _____ of robots" because they can do a lot more than the older ones could do.

3. A health coach robot can give health _____ such as: "Get more exercise today."

GETTING MEANING FROM CONTEXT

Find these sentences in "Robots Like Us." Match the bold words and expressions (1–3) with their meanings (a–c).

____ 1. Social robots can also **"read"** our facial expressions.

____ 2. Roboticists, like Cynthia Breazeal, believe that **it won't be long before** we have social robots in our homes, helping us live better lives.

____ 3. It speaks with a **synthesized** voice.

a. imitating something natural

b. understand using clues or hints

c. there soon will be a time when

CRITICAL THINKING

1. Evaluating. What do you think could be the pros and cons of using Autom? What advantages do you think Autom has compared to other weight-loss programs?

_____

_____

2. Reflecting. How would you use a social robot? Discuss your ideas with a partner.

_____

_____

EXPLORE MORE

Learn more about robots at nationalgeographic.com. Search for "robots." Find and bring to class pictures of different types of robots. Explain what they do.

TEDTALKS

THE RISE OF PERSONAL ROBOTS

CYNTHIA BREAZEAL Roboticist, TED speaker

🎧 Why do we have robots on Mars but not in our homes? This was a question Cynthia Breazeal asked herself when she was a graduate student at MIT in 1997.

Breazeal realized that robots are good at working with things, but not with people. So Breazeal decided to create a new kind of robot.

Today, Breazeal directs the Personal Robots Group at MIT's Media Lab. Her work focuses on building personal robots that are socially intelligent—robots that can interact and communicate with people. Breazeal is particularly interested in designing robots that can improve education, health, and communication. She has learned that the best designs "push our social buttons." In other words, people respond best to robots that communicate and interact with us in a similar way to humans. As Breazeal says, "Robots touch something deeply human within us."

In this lesson, you are going to watch segments of Breazeal's TED Talk. Use the information above to answer the questions.

1. What did Breazeal decide to do when she was a graduate student at MIT?

   _____

2. What are three aspects of life that Breazeal wants to improve with personal robots?

   _____

3. How do you think robots could improve those aspects of life?

   _____

   _____

Breazeal's **idea worth spreading** is that personal robots have the potential to improve our individual well-being and connect us more closely to one other.

A ROBOT SIDEKICK

PREVIEWING

A. **Read this excerpt from the first part of Breazeal's talk. What words do you think are missing? Complete each gap and share your ideas with a partner.**

    a. delight   **b.** exist   **c.** explore   **d.** interacted

« Ever since I was a little girl seeing *Star Wars* for the first time, I've been fascinated by this idea of personal robots. And as a little girl, I loved the idea of a robot that _____ with us much more like a helpful, trusted sidekick—something that would _____ us, enrich our lives, and help us save a galaxy or two. I knew robots like that didn't really _____, but I knew I wanted to build them.

So over the past several years, I've been continuing to _____ this interpersonal dimension of robots, now at the Media Lab with my own team of incredibly talented students. And one of my favorite robots is Leonardo. »

---

sidekick: *n.* a close friend or helper

enrich: *v.* add good things to

galaxy: *n.* a large system of stars

dimension: *n.* an aspect or feature of something

B. **Watch (▶) the first segment of the TED Talk, and check your answers to Exercise A.**

GETTING THE MAIN IDEA

Which statement best describes the main idea of this segment of the TED Talk?

a. You cannot create a robot like Leonardo without a large team of incredibly talented people.

b. If we build robots that communicate with us the way people do, they might be able to improve our lives.

c. We need to establish labs where we can create robots like the ones we see in movies like *Star Wars*.

UNDERSTANDING SEQUENCE

Breazeal shows a demonstration of how Leonardo works. Number the steps of the demonstration in the correct order from 1 to 7.

__7__ Leo looks afraid.

_____ Leo points to Cookie Monster.

_____ Leo looks at Cookie Monster and nods his head.

__1__ Matt says "Hello" to Leo. Leo "hears" Matt and nods his head.

_____ Matt tells Leo that Cookie Monster is very bad.

_____ Matt asks Leo, "Can you find Cookie Monster?"

_____ Matt shows Leo a puppet called "Cookie Monster."

Breazeal with the robot Leonardo.

MORE THAN A TOY

UNDERSTANDING MAIN IDEAS

A. Scan the following excerpt from the next part of Breazeal's TED Talk. With a partner, discuss your answers to these questions:

1. What family problem does Breazeal discuss?

2. How might a robot solve this problem?

“ Now let's try to put this into a little bit of context. Today we know that families are living farther and farther apart, and that definitely takes a toll on family relationships and family bonds over distance. For me, I have three young boys, and I want them to have a really good relationship with their grandparents. But my parents live thousands of miles away, so they just don't get to see each other that often. We try Skype, we try phone calls, but my boys are little—they don't really want to talk; they want to play. ”

---

takes a toll on: *v.* causes problems with

B. Watch (▶) this segment of the TED Talk. Were your answers for Exercise A correct?

UNDERSTANDING KEY DETAILS

Which statement in each pair best describes a key detail for this part of the TED talk?

1. **a.** Breazeal has created a robot that lets family members who live far away connect with each other.

   b. Breazeal wants to create a robot that lets family members who live far away connect with each other.

2. **a.** Breazeal's children are too young to Skype or talk on the phone.

   b. Because they are young, Breazeal's children prefer playing to talking.

3. **a.** Breazeal's "distance-play" technology will allow family members to play online with virtual toys.

   b. Breazeal's "distance-play" technology will allow family members to play together even if they're far away from each other.

SUMMARIZING

How does a grandma-bot work? Check (✓) the four best statements below.

☐ **1.** Grandma connects to a robot over the Internet.

☐ **2.** Grandma is in the same room as the children.

☐ **3.** The robot is connected to the children's computer.

☐ **4.** When Grandma picks up a toy, the robot picks up the same toy.

☐ **5.** The robot is in the same room as the children.

☐ **6.** The children see the robot on a computer screen.

CRITICAL THINKING

Analyzing. Can you think of any problems with using robots to communicate with family members?

_____

_____

EXPLORE MORE

Watch more of Breazeal's TED Talk at TED.com. How does Breazeal say that robots can help keep us healthy? Share your information with the class.

Project

A student builds a small robot in a research lab in the U.K.

A. Work with a partner. You are going to design a robot.

1. With your partner, decide the following:

   - What kind of robot is it (e.g., a social robot)?
   - What is its purpose?
   - Who does it help?
   - What does it look like?
   - What special skills does it have?

2. Create a two-minute presentation. Include a diagram or drawing of your robot.

B. Work with two other pairs.

- Give your presentations.
- As you listen, take notes.
- At the end, review your notes.
- Discuss: Which robot idea is the most useful? Why?

EXPLORE MORE

Learn more about robots. Go to TED.com and search for the playlist called "How to Live with Robots." Choose one of the TED Talks that interest you the most, and share what you learn with your class.

TEDTALK VIDEO TRANSCRIPTS

Unit 1

MATT CUTTS

Try Something New for 30 Days

A few years ago I felt like I was stuck in a rut, so I decided to follow in the footsteps of the great American philosopher, Morgan Spurlock, and try something new for 30 days. The idea is actually pretty simple. Think about something you've always wanted to add to your life, and try it for the next 30 days. It turns out, 30 days is just about the right amount of time to add a new habit or subtract a habit—like watching the news—from your life.

There's a few things I learned while doing these 30-day challenges. The first was, instead of the months flying by, forgotten, the time was much more memorable. This was part of a challenge I did to take a picture every day for a month. And I remember exactly where I was and what I was doing that day. I also noticed that as I started to do more and harder 30-day challenges, my self-confidence grew. I went from desk-dwelling computer nerd to the kind of guy who bikes to work—for fun. Even last year, I ended up hiking up Mt. Kilimanjaro, the highest mountain in Africa. I would never have been that adventurous before I started my 30-day challenges.

I also figured out that if you really want something badly enough, you can do anything for 30 days. Have you ever wanted to write a novel? Every November, tens of thousands of people try to write their own 50,000-word novel from scratch in 30 days. It turns out, all you have to do is write 1,667 words a day for a month. So I did. By the way, the secret is not to go to sleep until you've written your words for the day. You might be sleep-deprived, but you'll finish your novel. Now, is my book the next great American novel? No. I wrote it in a month. It's awful. But for the rest of my life, if I meet John Hodgman at a TED party, I don't have to say, "I'm a computer scientist." No, no. If I want to, I can say, "I'm a novelist."

So here's one last thing I'd like to mention. I learned that when I made small, sustainable changes, things I could keep doing, they were more likely to stick. There's nothing wrong with big, crazy challenges. In fact, they're a ton of fun. But they're less likely to stick. When I gave up sugar for 30 days, day 31 looked like this.

So here's my question to you: What are you waiting for? I guarantee you the next 30 days are going to pass whether you like it or not, so why not think about something you have always wanted to try, and give it a shot for the next 30 days.

Thanks.

Unit 2

TOM WUJEC

Build a Tower, Build a Team

Part 1

. . . So, normally, most people begin by orienting themselves to the task. They talk about it, they figure out what it's going to look like, they jockey for power. Then they spend some time planning, organizing, they sketch, and they lay out spaghetti. They spend the majority of their time assembling the sticks into ever-growing structures. And then, finally, just as they're running out of time, someone takes out the marshmallow, and then they gingerly put it on top, and then they stand back, and—ta-da!—they admire their work. But what really happens, most of the time, is that the "ta-da" turns into an "uh-oh," because the weight of the marshmallow causes the entire structure to buckle and to collapse.

Part 2

So there are a number of people who have a lot more "uh-oh" moments than others, and among the worst are recent graduates of business school. They lie, they cheat, they get distracted, and they produce really lame structures. And, of course, there are teams that have a lot more "ta-da" structures, and among the best are recent graduates of kindergarten. And it's pretty amazing. As Peter tells us, not only do they produce the tallest structures, but they're the most interesting structures of them all.

So the question you want to ask is: How come? Why? What is it about them? And Peter likes to say that none of the kids spend any time trying to be CEO of Spaghetti, Inc. Right? They don't spend time jockeying for power. But there's another reason as well. And the reason is that business students are trained to find the single right plan, right? And then they execute on it. And then what happens is, when they put the marshmallow on the top, they run out of time, and what happens? It's a crisis. Sound familiar? Right. What kindergarteners do differently is that they start with the marshmallow, and they build prototypes, successive

prototypes, always keeping the marshmallow on top, so they have multiple times to fix when they build prototypes along the way. Designers recognize this type of collaboration as the essence of the iterative process. And with each version, kids get instant feedback about what works and what doesn't work.

So the capacity to play in prototype is really essential, but let's look at how different teams perform. So the average for most people is around 20 inches; business school students, about half of that; lawyers, a little better, but not much better than that; kindergarteners, better than most adults. Who does the very best? Architects and engineers, thankfully. Thirty-nine inches is the tallest structure I've seen. And why is it? Because they understand triangles and self-reinforcing geometrical patterns are the key to building stable structures. So CEOs, a little bit better than average, but here's where it gets interesting. If you put you put an executive admin. on the team, they get significantly better. It's incredible. You know, you look around, you go, "Oh, that team's going to win." You can just tell beforehand. And why is that? Because they have special skills of facilitation. They manage the process, they understand the process. And any team who manages and pays close attention to work will significantly improve the team's performance. Specialized skills and facilitation skills are the combination that leads to strong success. If you have 10 teams that typically perform, you'll get maybe six or so that have standing structures. . . .

And the fundamental lesson, I believe, is that design truly is a contact sport. It demands that we bring all of our senses to the task and that we apply the very best of our thinking, our feeling, and our doing to the challenge that we have at hand. And sometimes, a little prototype of this experience is all that it takes to turn us from an "uh-oh" moment to a "ta-da" moment. And that can make a big difference.

Thank you very much.

This is an edited version of Wujec's 2010 TED Talk. To watch the full talk, visit TED.com.

DAVID GALLO
Underwater Astonishments

. . . That's the unknown world, and today we've only explored about three percent of what's out there in the ocean. Already we've found the world's highest mountains, the world's deepest valleys, underwater lakes, underwater waterfalls—a lot of that we shared with you from the stage. And in a place where we thought no life at all, we find more life, we think, and diversity and density than the tropical rainforest, which tells us that we don't know much about this planet at all. There's still 97 percent, and either that 97 percent is empty or just full of surprises.

But I want to jump up to shallow water now and look at some creatures that are positively amazing. Cephalopods—head-foots. As a kid I knew them as calamari, mostly. This is an octopus—this is the work of Dr. Roger Hanlon at the Marine Biological Lab—and it's just fascinating how cephalopods can, with their incredible eyes, sense their surroundings, look at light, look at patterns. Here's an octopus moving across the reef, finds a spot to settle down, curls up, and then disappears into the background. Tough thing to do.

In the next bit, we're going to see a couple squid. These are squid. Now males, when they fight, if they're really aggressive, they turn white. And these two males are fighting, they do it by bouncing their butts together, which is an interesting concept. Now, here's a male on the left and a female on the right, and the male has managed to split his coloration so the female only always sees the kinder gentler squid in him. And the male ... (Laughter) We're going to see it again. Let's take a look at it again. Watch the coloration: white on the right, brown on the left. He takes a step back — so he's keeping off the other males by splitting his body — and comes up on the other side ... Bingo! Now I'm told that's not just a squid phenomenon with males, but I don't know. (Laughter)

Cuttlefish. I love cuttlefish. This is a giant Australian cuttlefish. And there he is, his droopy little eyes up here. But they can do pretty amazing things, too. Here we're going to see one backing into a crevice, and watch his tentacles—he just pulls them in, makes them look just like algae. Disappears right into the background. Positively amazing. Here's two males fighting. Once again, they're smart enough, these cephalopods; they know not to hurt each other. But look at the patterns that they can do with their skin. That's an amazing thing.

Here's an octopus. Sometimes they don't want to be seen when they move because predators can see them. Here, this guy actually can make himself look like a rock, and, looking at his environment, can actually slide across the bottom, using the waves and the shadows so he can't be seen. His motion blends right into the background—the moving rock trick. So, we're learning lots new from the shallow water. Still exploring the deep, but learning lots from the shallow water. There's a good reason why: The shallow water's full of predators—here's a barracuda—and if you're an octopus or a cephalopod, you need to really understand how to use your surroundings to hide.

In the next scene, you're going to see a nice coral bottom. And you see that an octopus would stand out very easily there if you couldn't use your camouflage, use your skin to change color and texture. Here's some algae in the foreground . . . and an octopus. Ain't that amazing? Now, Roger spooked him so he took off in a cloud of ink, and when he lands, the octopus says, "Oh, I've been seen. The best thing to do is to get as big as I can get." That big brown makes his eyespot very big. So, he's bluffing. Let's do it backwards—I thought he was joking when he first showed it to me. I thought it was all graphics—so here it is in reverse. Watch the skin color; watch the skin texture. Just an amazing animal, it can change color and texture to match the surroundings. Watch him blend right into this algae. One, two, three. And now he's gone, and so am I.

Thank you very much.

This is an edited version of Gallo's 2007 TED Talk. To watch the full talk, visit TED.com.

JESSI ARRINGTON
Wearing Nothing New

Part 1

I'm Jessi, and this is my suitcase. But before I show you what I've got inside, I'm going to make a very public confession, and that is, I'm outfit-obsessed. I love finding, wearing, and more recently, photographing and blogging a different colorful, crazy outfit for every single occasion. But I don't buy anything new. I get all my clothes secondhand from flea markets and thrift stores. Aww, thank you. Secondhand shopping allows me to reduce the impact my wardrobe has on the environment and on my wallet. I get to meet all kinds of great people; my dollars usually go to a good cause; I look pretty unique; and it makes shopping like my own personal treasure hunt. I mean, what am I going to find today? Is it going to be my size? Will I like the color? Will it be under $20? If all the answers are yes, I feel as though I've won. . . .

So as I do this, I'm also going to tell you a few of the life lessons that, believe it or not, I have picked up in these adventures wearing nothing new.

Part 2

So let's start with Sunday. I call this "Shiny Tiger." You do not have to spend a lot of money to look great. You can almost always look phenomenal for under $50. This whole outfit, including the jacket, cost me $55, and it was the most expensive thing that I wore the entire week.

Monday: Color is powerful. It is almost physiologically impossible to be in a bad mood when you're wearing bright red pants. If you are happy, you are going to attract other happy people to you.

Tuesday: Fitting in is way overrated. I've spent a whole lot of my life trying to be myself and at the same time fit in. Just be who you are. If you are surrounding yourself with the right people, they will not only get it, they will appreciate it.

Wednesday: Embrace your inner child. Sometimes people tell me that I look like I'm playing dress-up, or that I remind them of their seven-year-old. I like to smile and say, "Thank you."

Thursday: Confidence is key. If you think you look good in something, you almost certainly do. And if you don't think you look good in something, you're also probably right. I grew up with a mom who taught me this day in and day out. But it wasn't until I turned 30 that I really got what this meant. And I'm going to break it down for you for just a second. If you believe you're a beautiful person inside and out, there is no look that you can't pull off. So there is no excuse for any of us here in this audience. We should be able to rock anything we want to rock. Thank you.

Friday: A universal truth—five words for you: Gold sequins go with everything.

And finally, Saturday: Developing your own unique personal style is a really great way to tell the world something about you without having to say a word. It's been proven to me time and time again as people have walked up to me this week simply because of what I'm wearing, and we've had great conversations.

So obviously this is not all going to fit back in my tiny suitcase. So before I go home to Brooklyn, I'm going to donate everything back. Because the lesson I'm trying to learn myself this week is that it's okay to let go. I don't need to get emotionally attached to these things because around the corner, there is always going to be another crazy, colorful, shiny outfit just waiting for me, if I put a little love in my heart and look.

Thank you very much.

This is an edited version of Arrington's 2011 TED Talk. To watch the full talk, visit TED.com.

CESAR KURIYAMA
One Second Every Day

Part 1

. . . So the first of those projects ended up being something I called "One Second Every Day." Basically, I'm recording one second of every day of my life for the rest of my life, chronologically compiling these one-second tiny slices of my life into one single continuous video until, you know, I can't record them anymore.

The purpose of this project is, one: I hate not remembering things that I've done in the past. There's all these things that I've done with my life that I have no recollection of unless someone brings it up, and sometimes I think, "Oh yeah. That's something that I did." And something that I realized early on in the project was that if I wasn't doing anything interesting, I would probably forget to record the video. So the day—the first time that I forgot, it really hurt me, because it's something that I really wanted to—from the moment that I turned 30, I wanted to keep this project going until forever, and having missed that one second, I realized, it just kind of created this thing in my head where I never forgot ever again.

So if I live to see 80 years of age, I'm going to have a five-hour video that encapsulates 50 years of my life. When I turn 40, I'll have a one-hour video that includes just my 30s. This has really invigorated me day-to-day, when I wake up, to try and do something interesting with my day.

Now, one of the things that I have issues with is that, as the days and weeks and months go by, time just seems to start blurring and blending into each other and, you know, I hated that, and visualization is the way to trigger memory. You know, this project for me is a way for me to bridge that gap and remember everything that I've done. Even just this one second allows me to remember everything else I did that one day. It's difficult, sometimes, to pick that one second. On a good day, I'll have maybe three or four seconds that I really want to choose, but I'll just have to narrow it down to one, but even narrowing it down to that one allows me to remember the other three anyway.

Part 2

. . . One of the reasons that I took my year off was to spend more time with my family, and this really tragic thing happened where my sister-in-law, her intestine suddenly strangled one day, and we took her to the emergency room, and she was, she was in really bad shape. We almost lost her a couple of times, and I was there with my brother every day. It helped me realize something else during this project, is that recording that one second on a really bad day is extremely difficult. It's not—we tend to take our cameras out when we're doing awesome things. Or we're, "Oh, yeah, this party, let me take a picture." But we rarely do that when we're having a bad day, and something horrible is happening. And I found that it's actually been very, very important to record even just that one second of a really bad moment. It really helps you appreciate the good times. It's not always a good day, so when you have a bad one, I think it's important to remember it, just as much as it is important to remember the [good] days.

Now one of the things that I do is, I don't use any filters, I don't use anything to—I try to capture the moment as much as possible as the way that I saw it with my own eyes. I started a rule of first-person perspective. Early on, I think I had a couple of videos where you would see me in it, but I realized that wasn't the way to go. The way to really remember what I saw was to record it as I actually saw it.

Now, a couple of things that I have in my head about this project are, wouldn't it be interesting if thousands of people were doing this? I turned 31 last week, which is there. I think it would be interesting to see what everyone did with a project like this. I think everyone would have a different interpretation of it. I think everyone would benefit from just having that one second to remember every day. Personally, I'm tired of forgetting, and this is a really easy thing to do. I mean, we all have HD-capable cameras in our pockets right now—most people in this room, I bet—and it's something that's—I never want to forget another day that I've ever lived, and this is my way of doing that, and it'd be really interesting also to see, if you could just type in on a website, "June 18, 2018," and you would just see a stream of people's lives on that particular day from all over the world.

And I don't know, I think this project has a lot of possibilities, and I encourage you all to record just a small snippet of your life every day, so you can never forget that that day, you lived.

Thank you.

This is an edited version of Kuriyama's 2012 TED Talk. To watch the full talk, visit TED.com.

IWAN BAAN

Ingenious Homes in Unexpected Places

Part 1

. . . Let's go now to Africa, to Nigeria, to a community called Makoko, a slum where 150,000 people live just meters above the Lagos Lagoon. While it may appear to be a completely chaotic place, when you see it from above, there seems to be a whole grid of waterways and canals connecting each and every home. From the main dock, people board long wooden canoes which carry them out to their various homes and shops located in the expansive area. When out on the water, it's clear that life has been completely adapted to this very specific way of living. Even the canoes become variety stores where ladies paddle from house to house, selling anything from toothpaste to fresh fruits. Behind every window and door frame, you'll see a small child peering back at you, and while Makoko seems to be packed with people, what's more shocking is actually the amount of children pouring out of every building. The population growth in Nigeria, and especially in these areas like Makoko, are painful reminders of how out of control things really are.

In Makoko, very few systems and infrastructures exist. Electricity is rigged, and freshest water comes from self-built wells throughout the area. This entire economic model is designed to meet a specific way of living on the water, so fishing and boat-making are common professions. . . .

On this particular evening, I came across this live band dressed to the T in their coordinating outfits. They were floating through the canals in a large canoe with a fitted-out generator for all of the community to enjoy. By nightfall, the area becomes almost pitch black, save for a small light bulb or a fire.

What originally brought me to Makoko was this project from a friend of mine, Kunlé Adeyemi, who recently finished building this three-story floating school for the kids in Makoko. With this entire village existing on the water, public space is very limited, so now that the school is finished, the ground floor is a playground for the kids, but when classes are out, the platform is just like a town square, where the fishermen mend their nets and floating shopkeepers dock their boats. . . .

Part 2

From Makoko to Zabbaleen, these communities have approached the tasks of planning, design, and management of their communities and neighborhoods in ways that respond specifically to their environment and circumstances. Created by these very people who live, work, and play in these particular spaces, these neighborhoods are intuitively designed to make the most of their circumstances.

In most of these places, the government is completely absent, leaving inhabitants with no choice but to re appropriate found materials, and while these communities are highly disadvantaged, they do present examples of brilliant forms of ingenuity, and prove that indeed we have the ability to adapt to all manner of circumstances. What makes places like the Torre David particularly remarkable is this sort of skeleton framework where people can have a foundation where they can tap into. Now imagine what these already ingenious communities could create themselves, and how highly particular their solutions would be if they were given the basic infrastructures that they could tap into.

Today, you see these large residential development projects which offer cookie-cutter housing solutions to massive amounts of people. From China to Brazil, these projects attempt to provide as many houses as possible, but they're completely generic and simply do not work as an answer to the individual needs of the people.

I would like to end with a quote from a friend of mine and a source of inspiration, Zita Cobb, the founder of the wonderful Shorefast Foundation, based out of Fogo Island, Newfoundland. She says that "there's this plague of sameness which is killing the human joy," and I couldn't agree with her more.

Thank you.

This is an edited version of Baan's 2013 TED Talk.
To watch the full talk, visit TED.com.

KEVIN ALLOCCA
Why Videos Go Viral

Part 1

Hi. I'm Kevin Allocca. I'm the trends manager at YouTube, and I professionally watch YouTube videos. It's true. So we're going to talk a little bit today about how videos go viral and then why that even matters. We all want to be stars—celebrities, singers, comedians—and when I was younger, that seemed so very, very hard to do. But now Web video has made it so that any of us or any of the creative things that we do can become completely famous in a part of our world's culture. Any one of you could be famous on the Internet by next Saturday. But there are over 48 hours of video uploaded to YouTube every minute. And of that, only a tiny percentage ever goes viral and gets tons of views and becomes a cultural moment. So how does it happen? Three things: tastemakers, communities of participation, and unexpectedness. All right, let's go.

[Video] **Bear Vasquez:** *Oh, my God. Oh, my God. Oh, my God! Wooo! Ohhhhh, wowwww!*

Last year, Bear Vasquez posted this video that he had shot outside his home in Yosemite National Park. In 2010, it was viewed 23 million times. This is a chart of what it looked like when it first became popular last summer. But he didn't actually set out to make a viral video, Bear . . .

And this video had actually been posted all the way back in January. So what happened here? Jimmy Kimmel, actually. Jimmy Kimmel posted this tweet that would eventually propel the video to be as popular as it would become. Because tastemakers like Jimmy Kimmel introduce us to new and interesting things and bring them to a larger audience.

Part 2

[Video] **Rebecca Black:** *It's Friday, Friday. Gotta get down on Friday. Everybody's looking forward to the weekend, weekend. Friday, Friday. Gettin' down on Friday.*

So you didn't think that we could actually have this conversation without talking about this video, I hope. Rebecca Black's "Friday" is one of the most popular videos of the year. It's been seen nearly 200 million times this year. This is a chart of what it looked like. And similar to "Double Rainbow," it seems to have just sprouted up out of nowhere.

So what happened on this day? Well, it was a Friday, this is true. And if you're wondering about those other spikes, those are also Fridays. But what about this day, this one particular Friday? Well, *Tosh.0* picked it up, a lot of blogs starting writing about it. Michael J. Nelson from *Mystery Science Theater* was one of the first people to post a joke about the video on Twitter. But what's important is that an individual or a group of tastemakers took a point of view and they shared that with a larger audience, accelerating the process.

And so then this community formed of people who shared this big inside joke and they started talking about it and doing things with it. And now there are 10,000 parodies of "Friday" on YouTube. Even in the first seven days, there was one parody for every other day of the week. Unlike the one-way entertainment of the 20th century, this community participation is how we become a part of the phenomenon—either by spreading it or by doing something new with it.

[Music] So "Nyan Cat" is a looped animation with looped music. It's this, just like this. It's been viewed nearly 50 million times this year. And if you think that that is weird, you should know that there is a three-hour version of this that's been viewed four million times. Even cats were watching this video. Cats were watching other cats watch this video.

But what's important here is the creativity that it inspired amongst this techie, geeky Internet culture. There were remixes. Someone made an old-timey version. And then it went international. An entire remix community sprouted up that brought it from being just a stupid joke to something that we can all actually be a part of. Because we don't just enjoy now, we participate.

Part 3

And who could have predicted any of this? Who could have predicted "Double Rainbow" or Rebecca Black or "Nyan Cat"? What scripts could you have written that would have contained this in it? In a world where over two days of video get uploaded every minute, only that which is truly unique and unexpected can stand out in the way that these things have. When a friend of mine told me that I needed to see this great video about a guy protesting bicycle fines in New York City, I admit I wasn't very interested.

[Video] **Casey Niestat:** *So I got a ticket for not riding in the bike lane, but often there are obstructions that keep you from properly riding in the bike lane.*

By being totally surprising and humorous, Casey Niestat got his funny idea and point seen 5 million times. And so this approach holds for anything new that we do creatively. And so it all brings us to one big question ...

[Video] **Bear Vasquez:** *What does this mean? Ohhhh.*

What does it mean? Tastemakers, creative participating communities, complete unexpectedness, these are characteristics of a new kind of media and a new kind of culture where anyone has access, and the audience defines the popularity. . . .

This is an edited version of Allocca's 2011 TED Talk. To watch the full talk visit TED.com.

RICHARD TURERE
My Invention that Made Peace with Lions

Part 1

This is where I live. I live in Kenya, at the south parts of the Nairobi National Park. Those are my dad's cows at the back, and behind the cows, that's the Nairobi National Park. Nairobi National Park is not fenced in the south widely, which means wild animals like zebras migrate out of the park freely. So predators like lions follow them, and this is what they do. They kill our livestock. This is one of the cows which was killed at night, and I just woke up in the morning and I found it dead, and I felt so bad, because it was the only bull we had. . . .

So I had to find a way of solving this problem. And the first idea I got was to use fire, because I thought lions were scared of fire. But I came to realize that that didn't really help, because it was even helping the lions to see through the cowshed. So I didn't give up. I continued.

And a second idea I got was to use a scarecrow. I was trying to trick the lions [into thinking] that I was standing near the cowshed. But lions are very clever. They will come the first day and they see the scarecrow, and they go back, but the second day, they'll come and they say, this thing is not moving here, it's always here. So he jumps in and kills the animals.

So one night, I was walking around the cowshed with a torch, and that day, the lions didn't come. And I discovered that lions are afraid of a moving light. So I had an idea.

Part 2

Since I was a small boy, I used to work in my room for the whole day, and I even took apart my mom's new radio, and that day she almost killed me, but I learned a lot about electronics. So I got an old car battery, [and] an indicator box. It's a small device found in a motorcycle, and it helps motorists when they want to turn right or left. It blinks. And I got a switch where I can switch on the lights, on and off. And that's a small torch from a broken flashlight.

So I set up everything. As you can see, the solar panel charges the battery, and the battery supplies the power to the small indicator box. I call it a transformer. And the indicator box makes the lights flash. As you can see, the bulbs face outside, because that's where the lions come from. And that's how it looks to lions when they come at night. The lights flash and trick the lions into thinking I was walking around the cowshed, but I was sleeping in my bed. Thanks.

So I set it up in my home two years ago, and since then, we have never experienced any problem with lions. And my neighboring homes heard about this idea. One of them was this grandmother. She had a lot of her animals being killed by lions, and she asked me if I could put the lights for her. And I said, "Yes." So I put the lights. You can see at the back, those are the lion lights. Since now, I've set up seven homes around my community, and they're really working. And my idea is also being used now all over Kenya for scaring other predators like hyenas, leopards, and it's also being used to scare elephants away from people's farms. . . .

I used to hate lions, but now because my invention is saving my father's cows and the lions, we are able to stay with the lions without any conflict. *Ashê olên.* It means in my language, thank you very much.

This is an edited version of Turere's 2013 TED Talk. To watch the full talk, visit TED.com.

CANDY CHANG

Before I Die, I Want to . . .

Part 1

There are a lot of ways the people around us can help improve our lives. We don't bump into every neighbor, so a lot of wisdom never gets passed on, though we do share the same public spaces. . . .

I live near this house, and I thought about how I could make it a nicer space for my neighborhood, and I also thought about something that changed my life forever.

In 2009, I lost someone I loved very much. Her name was Joan, and she was a mother to me, and her death was sudden and unexpected. And I thought about death a lot, and this made me feel deep gratitude for the time I've had, and brought clarity to the things that are meaningful to my life now. But I struggle to maintain this perspective in my daily life. I feel like it's easy to get caught up in the day-to-day, and forget what really matters to you.

So, with help from old and new friends, I turned the side of this abandoned house into a giant chalkboard and stenciled it with a fill-in-the-blank sentence: "Before I die, I want to . . . " So anyone walking by can pick up a piece of chalk, reflect on their lives, and share their personal aspirations in public space.

I didn't know what to expect from this experiment, but by the next day, the wall was entirely filled out, and it kept growing. And I'd like to share a few things that people wrote on this wall.

Part 2

"Before I die, I want to be tried for piracy." "Before I die, I want to straddle the International Date Line." "Before I die, I want to sing for millions." "Before I die, I want to plant a tree." "Before I die, I want to live off the grid." "Before I die, I want to hold her one more time." "Before I die, I want to be someone's cavalry." "Before I die, I want to be completely myself."

So, this neglected space became a constructive one, and people's hopes and dreams made me laugh out loud, tear up, and they consoled me during my own tough times. It's about knowing you're not alone. It's about understanding our neighbors in new and enlightening ways. It's about making space for reflection and contemplation, and remembering what really matters most to us as we grow and change.

I made this last year, and started receiving hundreds of messages from passionate people who wanted to make a wall with their community, so my civic center colleagues and I made a tool kit, and now walls have been made in countries around the world, including Kazakhstan, South Africa, Australia, Argentina, and beyond. Together, we've shown how powerful our public spaces can be if we're given the opportunity to have a voice and share more with one another. . . .

Our shared spaces can better reflect what matters to us as individuals and as a community, and with more ways to share our hopes, fears, and stories, the people around us can not only help us make better places, they can help us lead better lives. Thank you.

This is an edited version of Chang's 2012 TED Talk. To watch the full talk, visit TED.com.

Unit 10

CYNTHIA BREAZEAL

The Rise of Personal Robots

Part 1

Ever since I was a little girl seeing *Star Wars* for the first time, I've been fascinated by this idea of personal robots. And as a little girl, I loved the idea of a robot that interacted with us much more like a helpful, trusted sidekick—something that would delight us, enrich our lives, and help us save a galaxy or two. I knew robots like that didn't really exist, but I knew I wanted to build them. . . .

So over the past several years I've been continuing to explore this interpersonal dimension of robots, now at the Media Lab with my own team of incredibly talented students. And one of my favorite robots is Leonardo. We developed Leonardo in collaboration with Stan Winston Studio. And so I want to show you a special moment for me of Leo. This is Matt Berlin interacting with Leo, introducing Leo to a new object. And because it's new, Leo doesn't really know what to make of it. But sort of like us, he can actually learn about it from watching Matt's reaction.

[Video] **Matt Berlin**: Hello, Leo. Leo, this is Cookie Monster. Can you find Cookie Monster? Leo, Cookie Monster is very bad. He's very bad, Leo. Cookie Monster is very, very bad. He's a scary monster. He wants to get your cookies. . . .

So what I've learned through building these systems is that robots are actually a really intriguing social technology, where it's actually their ability to push our social buttons and to interact with us like a partner that is a core part of their functionality. And with that shift in thinking, we can now start to imagine new questions, new possibilities for robots that we might not have thought about otherwise. But what do I mean when I say "push our social buttons"? Well, one of the things that we've learned is that, if we design these robots to communicate with us using the same body language, the same sort of non-verbal cues that people use—like Nexi, our humanoid robot, is doing here—what we find is that people respond to robots a lot like they respond to people. People use these cues to determine things like how persuasive someone is, how likable, how engaging, how trustworthy. It turns out it's the same for robots. . . .

Part 2

Now let's try to put this into a little bit of context. Today we know that families are living further and further apart, and that definitely takes a toll on family relationships and family bonds over distance. For me, I have three young boys, and I want them to have a really good relationship with their grandparents. But my parents live thousands of miles away, so they just don't get to see each other that often. We try Skype, we try phone calls, but my boys are little—they don't really want to talk; they want to play. So I love the idea of thinking about robots as a new kind of distance-play technology. I imagine a time not too far from now—my mom can go to her computer, open up a browser and jack into a little robot. And as Grandma-bot, she can now play, really play, with my sons, with her grandsons, in the real world with his real toys. I could imagine grandmothers being able to do social-plays with their granddaughters, with their friends, and to be able to share all kinds of other activities around the house, like sharing a bedtime story. And through this technology, being able to be an active participant in their grandchildren's lives in a way that's not possible today. . . .

Robots touch something deeply human within us. And so whether they're helping us to become creative and innovative, or whether they're helping us to feel more deeply connected despite distance, or whether they are our trusted sidekick who's helping us attain our personal goals in becoming our highest and best selves, for me, robots are all about people.

Thank you.

This is an edited version of Breazeal's 2010 TED Talk. To watch the full talk, visit TED.com.

VOCABULARY LOG

As you complete each unit, use this chart to record definitions and example sentences of key vocabulary. Add other useful words or phrases you learn.

Unit	Vocabulary	Definition/Example
1	attitude *	
	experience	
	goal *	
	impact *	
	individual *	
	inspire	
	positive *	
	project *	
	_____	
2	designer *	
	expert *	
	plan	
	product	
	stable *	
	structure *	
	successful	
	tower	
	_____	
3	amazing	
	attractive	
	blend in	
	fierce	
	liquid	
	pattern	
	search	
	skin	
	_____	
4	behavior	
	creative *	
	luck	
	pay attention	
	perform	
	point out	
	style *	
	uniform *	
	_____	
5	camera	
	equipment *	
	image *	
	look after	
	precious	
	preserve	
	record	
	responsible	
	_____	

Unit	Vocabulary	Definition/Example
6	community *	
	construction *	
	encourage	
	materials	
	professional *	
	resident *	
	technique *	
	unique *	
7	definition *	
	expect	
	make sense	
	post	
	predict *	
	sensation	
	suddenly	
	talent	
8	afraid	
	benefit *	
	conflict *	
	government	
	migrate *	
	solve	
	take seriously	
	wild	
9	initiative	
	message	
	neighborhood	
	print	
	public	
	reach out	
	reaction *	
	abandoned *	
10	advice	
	develop	
	emotion	
	express	
	generation *	
	interact *	
	motivate	
	respond *	

* These words are on the Academic Word List (AWL), a list of the 570 most frequent word families in academic texts. The AWL does not include words that are among the most frequent 2,000 words of English. For more information, see www.victoria.ac.nz/lals/resources/academicwordlist/

Text Credits

Text credits: **66–67** Adapted from "Bill Bonner: the Archivist of Photographic Memories," by Kathryn Carlson: proof.nationalgeographic.com, Jan 2014; **108–109** Adapted from "The Kitengela Six–Outrage Over Lion Killings in Nairobi," by Dr. Paula Kahumbu: National Geographic News, Jun 21, 2012

Image Credits

8–9 ©R. Tyler Gross/Getty Images. **10–11** ©Michael Brands/TED. **12** (tl) ©Kylie Dunn. **13** (t) ©David Clare/First Light Photography. **15** (b) ©Matt Dunn. 16–17 © James Duncan Davidson / TED. **18** (b) ©Robert Clark/National Geographic Creative. **20** (t) ©Harvey Lloyd/Getty Images. **22–23** ©Bjorn Svensson/Age Fotostock. **24–25** © Sandra Hudson–Knapp/Getty Images. **26** (b) ©Tom Wujec. **27** (t) © Exploratorium. www.exploratorium.edu. **30–31** ©Ryan Lash/TED. **32** (b) ©Tom Wujec. **33** (b) ©Tom Wujec. **35** (cl) ©Corbis/Fotolia LLC, **35** (cbl) ©Marek Walica /Fotolia LLC, **35** (c) ©Visualcortex/Fotolia LLC, **35** (cbr) ©Andrey Kuzmin/Fotolia LLC, **35** (cr) ©FedotovAnatoly/Fotolia LLC, **35** (bl) ©National Geographic Learning, **35** (bcl) ©Mexrix/Fotolia LLC, **35** (bc) ©Mariontxa/Fotolia LLC, **35** (bcr) ©Kornienko/Fotolia LLC, **35** (br) ©Peter Hansen/Shutterstock.com. **36–37** ©BRIAN J. SKERRY/National Geographic Creative. **38–39** © CARRIE VONDERHAAR/OCEAN FUTURES SOCIETY/National Geographic Creative. **40** (b) ©Nature/UIG/Getty Images, **40** (inset) ©BRIAN J. SKERRY/National Geographic Creative, **40** (tr) ©Mapping Specialists, Ltd. Madison, WI USA. **41** (t) ©Nature/UIG/Getty Images. **43** (br) © Andre Seale/SpecialistStock/Aurora Photos. **44–45** ©Robert Leslie/TED. **46** (t) ©Philippe Bourseiller/Getty Images. **49** (t) ©davidmocholi/Getty Images. **50–51** ©Melissa Farlow/National Geographic Creative. **52–53** TAYLOR KENNEDY/National Geographic Creative. **54** (tr) © Jessica Quirk. **57** (bl) ©Emmanuel Faure/Getty Images. **58–59** ©Michael Brands/TED. **61** (c) ©Michael Brands/TED. **63** (t) ©Sandy Huffaker/Reuters. **64–65** ©H.E. Park/National Geographic Creative. **66–67** ©Oscar D. Von Engeln/National Geographic Creative. **68** (bl) ©Maridav/Shutterstock.com. **69** (t) ©Edwin Levick/National Geographic Creative. **71** (b) ©Adrian Coakley/National Geographic Creative. **73** ©James Duncan Davidson/TED. **75** (br) ©1000 Words/Shutterstock.com. **77** (t) ©Adrianko/Alamy. **78–79** ©Iwan Baan. **80–81** ©ZJAN/Mandatory Credit: WENN.com/Newscom. **82** (b) ©BNKR Arquitectura/solent, **82** (inset) ©Mapping Specialists, Ltd. Madison, WI USA. **83** (t) ©Michael Stravato/New York Times/Redux. **87** ©James Duncan Davidson/TED. **88** (t) ©Iwan Baan, **88** (inset) ©Mapping Specialists, Ltd. Madison, WI USA. **91** (t) ©JoeCornish/Arcaid/Architecture/Corbis. **92–93** ©Lars Howlett/Aurora Photos. **94–95** ©scyther5/Shutterstock.com. **96** (b) ©Cenveo® Publisher Services, **96** (inset) ©ZUMA Press. Inc/Alamy. **99** (tr) ©Isaac Brekken/Getty Images. 101 ©Ryan Lash/TED. **102** (t) ©Bettmann/CORBIS. **105** (t) ©Eric Whitacre/Virtual Choir. **106–107** ©Anup Shah/Terra/Corbis. **108–109** ©MICHAEL NICHOLS/National Geographic Creative. **110** (b) ©**National Geographic Maps. 111** (t) ©Peter Macdiarmid/Getty Images. **114–115** ©James Duncan Davidson/TED. **116** (t) ©Brent Stirton/Reportage by Getty Images. **118** (t) ©NGL Design. **119** (t) Gavriel Jecan/Terra/Corbis. **120–121** ©Alexandra Pucharelli. **122–123** ©Candy Chang. 124 (b) ©Candy Chang, **124** (inset) ©Mapping Specialists, Ltd. Madison, WI USA. **125** (t) ©Kris Davidson/National Geographic Creative. **127** (b) ©Candy Chang. **129** ©James Duncan Davidson/TED. **130** (t) ©Stringer Mexico/Reuters. **133** (t) ©Adam Berry/Getty Images. **134–135** ©Lu Yan/Imagechina. **136–137** ©Mikey Siegel/Personal Robots Group/M.I.T. Media Lab. **138** (br) ©Adam Hunger/Reuters. **139** (t) ©United Archives GmbH/Alamy. **140** (cl) ©Mikey Siegel/Personal Robots Group/M.I.T. Media Lab, 140 (cr) ©Adam Hunger/Reuters. **143** ©James Duncan Davidson/TED. **145** (tr) ©Sam Ogden/Science Source. **147** (t) ©Peter Cade/Iconica/Getty Images

Acknowledgements

The Authors and Publisher would like to thank the following teaching professionals for their valuable input during the development of this series:

Carlos Budding, Akita International University; **Amy Cook,** Bowling Green State University; **Jay Klaphake,** Ritsumeikan University; **Anthony Lavigne,** Kansai Gaidai University; **Jeremy Lindeck,** ACE; **Susan Swier,** Educational Consultant; **Anya Van Elderen,** Grand Rapids Community College; **Erin Wynn,** Johnson & Wales University; **Sarah Worthington,** Educational Consultant

And special thanks to: Iwan Baan, Candy Chang, Kylie Dunn, Jessica Quirk, Tom Wujec, Eric Whitacre, Mary Kadera and the Personal Robots Group at MIT Media Lab.